HIDE

NMAI EDITIONS

National Museum of the American Indian

Smithsonian Institution

Washington and New York

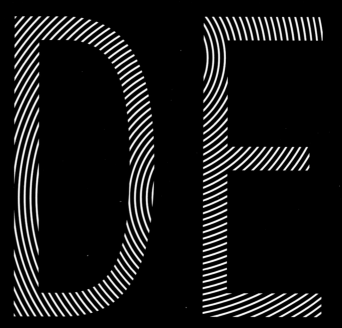

HIDE

SKIN AS MATERIAL
AND METAPHOR

Edited by
Kathleen Ash-Milby

The National Museum of the American Indian, Smithsonian Institution, is dedicated to working in collaboration with the indigenous peoples of the Americas to foster and protect Native cultures throughout the Western Hemisphere. The museum's publishing program seeks to augment awareness of Native American beliefs and lifeways and to educate the public about the history and significance of Native cultures.

Associate Director for Museum Programs
Tim Johnson

Head of Publications
Tanya Thrasher, Acting

Content Editor
Kathleen Ash-Milby

Copy Editor
Alexandra Harris

Senior Designer
Steve Bell

Editorial Assistance
Jane McAllister, Amy Pickworth, and Liz Hill

First Edition
10 9 8 7 6 5 4 3 2 1

For more information about the Smithsonian's National Museum of the American Indian, visit the NMAI website at www.AmericanIndian.si.edu. To support the museum by becoming a member, call 1-800-242-NMAI (6624) or click on "Support" on our website.

Published in conjunction with the exhibition *HIDE: Skin as Material and Metaphor*, on view from March 2010 to January 2011 at the NMAI's George Gustav Heye Center.

Library of Congress Cataloging-in-Publication Data
Hide : skin as material and metaphor / edited by Kathleen Ash-Milby.—1st ed.
    p. cm.
Published in conjunction with an exhibition on view at the National Museum of the American Indian, New York, NY, Mar. 2010–Jan. 2011.
Includes bibliographical references.
ISBN 978-1-933565-15-6 (alk. paper)
1. Indian art—North America—21st century—Exhibitions. 2. Art, American—21st century—Exhibitions. 3. Indians of North America—Ethnic identity—Exhibitions. 4. Ethnicity in art—Exhibitions. I. Ash-Milby, Kathleen E. II. National Museum of the American Indian (U.S.) III. Title: Skin as material and metaphor.
N6538.A4H48 2009
704.03'970074753–dc22
                    2009051061

Cover: Sonya Kelliher-Combs, *Red Reindeer Brand*, 2009. Reindeer fur, acrylic polymer, cotton fabric, and metal grommets, 61 x 45.7 cm. Collection of the artist.

Title page: Arthur Renwick, *Carla*, 2006. Digital print (artist's proof, ed. of 3), 119.4 x 114.3 cm. Collection of the artist.

CONTENTS

"A Thick-Skinned Beast"

Being Indian, looking Indian, playing Indian—they are all about surface appearances, what they reveal, and what they hide. But they are also about what we choose to see.

—Kathleen Ash-Milby

American Indians are often masters of metaphor. Alternative meanings that reflect our spirituality and the histories and narratives of our communities charge much of the world around us. This also extends to the artwork we create. There is no great mystery inherent to any of this, of course, nor are Native people unique in this way. It is a symptom of the human condition to crave and create meaning, to examine and interpret what we've been presented with, and to make choices about what we reveal or hide or see.

It's also no surprise that skin—our most intimate cover for what's literally on the inside of each of us—offers rich material in terms of metaphor. The English language presents a number of examples related to skin that we use without thought, almost daily. Some are cautionary words about illusion and reality, as in *beauty is only skin deep*. Other phrases—*it's like a second skin* or *it got under my skin*—suggest comfort, or the lack of it. And descriptors like *thick skinned* or *thin skinned* speak of the emotional distance we maintain between ourselves and others. The same multilayered nature of the artworks in *HIDE: Skin as Material and Metaphor* is central not only to the exhibition but to this book's essays. The exhibition—the name of which offers its own multiple meanings—assembles the work of several contemporary artists as they examine issues of identity and consider what it means to be Indian within the context of what we choose to reveal, to hide, and to see.

As individuals, our skin is not only a protection but also a document of our wounds and healing, a witness to our personal histories in the form of scars, stretch marks, and wrinkles. Maori, Hawaiian, and other traditional indigenous tattoo designs literally inscribe an individual's story and life force on the skin, and many people today find it appropriate to express themselves by ornamenting their bodies with tattoos, makeup and other forms of paint, and piercings. These alterations aside (and despite American culture's apparent obsession with preventing or treating signs of aging), we generally expect an individual's skin to accurately represent their life experiences. After all, to be truly unimpeded by the confines of our histories, as documented in the form of our skin, is to belong to the indigenous realm of shapeshifters, those who possess supernatural abilities to change their physical form. At the end of the day, our skin keeps us honest. Try as we might, we cannot separate ourselves from it. And we should not want to.

Our "hides" are important to this dialogue as well. Entire communities may become defined, by themselves and others, based on what they collectively decide to reveal or keep hidden. Another significant conversation about identity and self determination is currently underway at the National Museum of the American Indian, in partnership with the National Museum of African American History and Culture, in the form of the exhibition *IndiVisible* and its related scholarship. Like *HIDE*, *IndiVisible* considers surface appearances, and what they reveal and hide, within the specific context of our African-Native American communities.

Our "red" skin has meant a great many things to us and to others over the last several centuries. It has been venerated and nearly idolized, and it has made us vulnerable to hate and violence. It has been a source of pride and shame and confusion within our communities, especially as related to its various shades, which themselves bear witness to the various histories of our ancestors. And for as long as Native people have been recorded in images, we have been misrepresented, whether in the beautifully staged romantic photographs by Edward S. Curtis, the perverse exaggerations of sports mascots and Hollywood stereotypes, or the unintentional distortions by otherwise well-meaning individuals. The deconstruction of this imagery is central to *HIDE*. Here we ponder the artists' representations of a few of the many ways of being a "real" twenty-first-century Indian: celebrating our beautiful skin, acknowledging the scars we bear as individuals and as tribal nations, and recognizing the scars we inflict on our Mother Earth. *HIDE* is also a manifestation of a larger and long-term initiative at the National Museum of the American Indian, namely its Modern and Contemporary Native Arts Program, which will continue to present thoughtful and innovative works by today's leading Indian artists.

I am reminded of the words of American poet Walt Whitman—himself a master of metaphor—who once said, "The public is a thick-skinned beast, and you have to keep whacking away at its hide to let it know you're there." I'm grateful to the artists who continue to whack away, and in the process have enlightened us about who they—and who we all—are.

Kevin Gover (Pawnee)
Director, National Museum of the American Indian

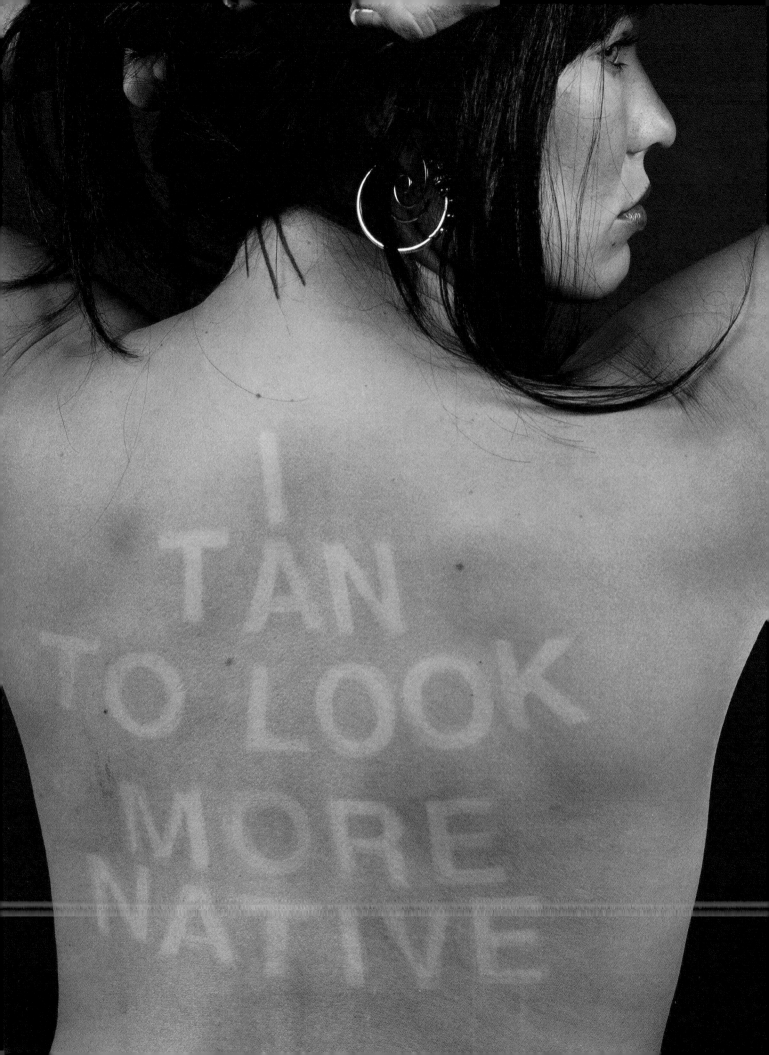

Under My Skin, Deep in the Heart of Me

Erica Lord (Athabascan/Inupiat),
I Tan to Look More Native (detail),
2006. Digital print, 10.2 x 12.7 cm.

A double meaning is at play here in *HIDE,* this exhibition's title. There is a literal, *material* hide—whether buffalo, deer, or walrus—and the reference to that which is *hidden,* under the radar screen, disguised, out of view. Over the years, the National Museum of the American Indian (NMAI) has presented many works that incorporate "hides" in a literal sense, such as the exhibition *Identity by Design: Tradition, Change, and Celebration in Native Women's Dresses* (2007–09), or exhibitions that feature complex contemporary art, requiring a close look to see the *hidden meaning.* In particular, one section of *Identity by Design* included dresses worn for the Ghost Dance, which revealed something deeper about our history that transcends what can be expressed through the written word. *In looking at these dresses made from hides, we can see that which is hidden.* The NMAI's exhibition *First American Art: The Charles and Valerie Diker Collection of American Indian Art* (2004–05) featured incredible drawings on the pages of ledger books by Native artists in the late nineteenth century. Once buffalo hides were unavailable, these artists turned to the pages of accounting books from non-Native military officers as a substitute for drawing directly on an animal skin to record key events in tribal history. The hide was no longer the primary canvas for the Native artist.

In 2007, Erica Lord's work was featured in a solo exhibition, *Definitions of the Exotic,* curated by Sarah Sense for the American Indian Community House Gallery in New York City. The signature image for the show was a provocative photographic self-portrait of the artist in half-torso with her back in close range. Using an adhesive tape to create this work, she tanned her back and then removed the tape for the shot; the words "I Tan to Look More Native" appeared on her back in bold block letters where the tape had been. Who was the Hidden One who put the tape on the artist's back so we onlookers could read her words? Was the artist commenting on what it means when the lighter skinned take special measures to become darker skinned by spending hours in tanning salons or the bright sunlight? What are the cultural perceptions of leisure, race, identity, and how is all this tied to the colors of our hides?

Lord challenges the viewers' assumptions and their cultural reading of the image: what is the artist's ethnic identity? Isn't identity a culturally constructed idea of just who is and who isn't a "real" Indian? Is her skin pigment "dark enough" to qualify? The viewer may assume that the artist is of mixed heritage, and the question of her blood quantum may come to mind. In contrast to more permanent changes to the body, such as tattoos and body piercings, the tanned and untanned areas on her body are temporary and transient. This, of course, is the subtext of the piece. The work is simultaneously confrontational and deeply personal and expressive. It touches on complex political and social issues, and yet it is skillfully rendered and visually arresting. The artist proclaims, "Look at me," while subtly suggesting that we viewers take a closer look at others and the complexity of their individual projections of cultural identity.

HIDE's curator, Kathleen Ash-Milby (Navajo), has organized a complex exhibition that illuminates the surface of, or just beneath, issues critical to both Native and non-Native viewers. This exhibition explores the intricacies of art making while incorporating the use of skin and hide both as material and metaphor to advocate going beyond that which is skin deep. Both meanings of "hide"—as commodity and idea—serve as raw material for Native artists. Ash-Milby's curatorial decisions address multiple layers of skin—the exterior that protects us from the elements yet is vulnerable and can be punctured or otherwise altered. Animal skins wrapped around us can provide warmth, project a fantasy of grandeur, or mask us. Our own skins, weathered by age, the elements of wind and sun, and too many cigarettes reveal our stories in ways that words cannot even begin to express. The tundra and other landscapes on our planet are arguably surfaces that form a kind of skin for Mother Earth.

The exhibition is organized into four parts, the first three comprising solo artist installations and the fourth a group photography installation. The three installation artists—Sonya Kelliher-Combs (Inupiaq/Athabascan), Nadia Myre (Anishinaabe), and Michael Belmore (Ojibway)—are all sophisticated artists who incorporate their individual cultural histories into their artistic production yet bring a solid understanding of contemporary cultural context to the table. Using a variety of both traditional and nontraditional source materials, they manipulate their media with great skill and craftsmanship. The results are dazzling, politically charged, culturally meaningful, and quite dramatic, incorporating repetition, ritual, and risk into their work. The artists practice a form of social participation (whether with people or one's direct encounter with the natural world) in order to produce their art. Their work expresses both an appreciation of the beauty of daily life and an understanding of the elements they use, along with the particular challenges and constraints of enlisting social participation as the core of their artistic practice. In what is arguably an era of the spectacle of large media-driven public events, they understand an aesthetic practice that is both intimate and dependant on physical gestures. The creation of the art installations in this exhibition is highly interactive (with land, with people, with materials, and certainly in the act of making the work itself). This work calls upon us not as idle observers but as viewers fully engaged in the dynamism of what we behold. There is a performative quality used by these artists in terms of production; this is clear evidence of the physicality of the art.

The photography installation artists—Arthur Renwick (Haisla), KC Adams (Métis), Rosalie Favell (Cree Métis), Sarah Sense (Chitimacha/Choctaw), and Terrance Houle (Blood)—use portraiture to challenge our cultural assumptions about identity, stereotype, the gestures embedded in posing, skin color, and highly stylized ideas about the self and the other, social marginalization, and the social and cultural visualizations that project "Native-ness" (or not). Arthur Renwick focuses on the physical manipulation of the face to convey a range of emotions head-on. KC Adams's *Cyborg Hybrids* forces us to consider our cultural attitudes and assumptions about Indian people of mixed heritage, as if to ask, "Who really is an Indian?" By using highly stereotyped poses, she "captures" her subjects within the image much as prominent white male photographers did in historical photographs of Indians during the late nineteenth and early twentieth centuries. Rosalie Favell's portraits show Native people with an honest directness that reveals their humanity and their connectedness both to their communities and the larger society. Indians need not be in full regalia to be completely and totally Indian. Terrance Houle's *Urban Indian Series* includes images of himself in full regalia doing ordinary activities like going to the grocery store, taking a bath, getting dressed in the morning, or interacting with casually dressed urbanites. Sarah Sense masterfully uses weaving techniques to speak about cultural representation and projections through a highly patterned visual style. Together, these photographers bring forth an understanding about the interplay of popular culture, representation, and historic traditions.

For this publication, Ash-Milby invited a diverse group of cultural historians and critics to contribute essays about the artists and put their work in a broader cultural context, in terms of both contemporary Native American art and a global perspective. In the first chapter, Ash-Milby presents an overview of many of the complex issues surrounding the concept of skin for Native people, as a material with a long cultural history and as a visual icon loaded with meaning and misrepresentation. She also introduces us to each of the artists featured in the exhibition, describing how the work she selected uses the concept of skin as a material or as a metaphor for a myriad of issues.

Art historian Aleta Ringlero (Pima) discusses Sonya Kelliher-Combs's complex, densely layered, and intimate work. She reminds us that the artist's ideas about Native cultural identity are central to her creations, but then so is her understanding of that which is cosmopolitan. There is a sense of tragic, emotionally charged personal loss evident in Kelliher-Combs's art, which, though informed by older traditions of her community, also reflects contemporary concerns. The artist's work has an eloquence that is coupled with a reluctance to be explicit. This quality makes her installations quite powerful and expressive. Her work incorporates many cultural references, signs, and symbols, and certainly investigates complex subjects. The manipulation of the materials, especially on the surfaces (scratched, added to, and dug into), carries the meaning of her work into a new terrain. Her art not only examines her self, it reclaims it.

Anne Ellegood brings a deeply informed understanding about modern and contemporary art to her essay about Nadia Myre. Ellegood asserts that art making is really a form of language and that the featured artists in *HIDE* are not strictly making art, but rather are engaged in a high level of investigation drawn from their individual histories. Ellegood regards Myre as an artist who calls upon her personal biography to make work that is deeply self-referential. Like abstract expressionism, so much concerns the artist's signature brush stroke or gesture. Myre's work incorporates broad gestures in its realization, requiring extensive physical labor and repetition combined with a raw and direct pull from her life experience. Dale McConathy, one of my mentors when I was an adjunct professor at New York University, held the view that all art, even in its most conceptual or abstract form, is essentially about documentation, autobiography, and sometimes both. Using this definition, Myre's work undoubtedly falls into both camps.

In his essay, Ihor Holubizky writes that sculptor Michael Belmore works both in "slow tempo" and in a visual language completely his own. His work doesn't reference collective identity; rather, it is about an expression of a world he has come to know from experience. Belmore uses rivers, streams, wetlands, and the shoreline as artistic source materials. His work expresses tremendous energy through the highly physical acts of carving raw materials, assembling rocks and stones in situ, and even boldly hammering the elements like sheets of copper. Holubizky sees Belmore more as an artist who explains the world he knows through his work, in contrast to artists who incorporate nature to make more monumental creations. Belmore understands the intersection of land and water, their surfaces and rhythms, and expresses an informed knowledge of the effects of human activity on the landscape.

The essay by Jolene Rickard (Tuscarora) gives special focus to the Native photographers in the exhibition, in particular concerning the dialogue presented through art and exhibitions. Rickard is deeply engaged in the discourse about cultural negotiations and indigeneity (how indigenous people express their cultures and lives, both within and outside their communities). She writes that "focus on the exterior surface not only creates a space for interior illumination for the individual artist but also provides a glimpse into contemporary indigenous musings." Rickard speaks of the "mapping of skin" as a particular colonial construct that the photographers in the exhibition reject, renegotiate, or expand upon. In very deliberate ways, Native people are continually negotiating place and space, their histories, and the present. She also reminds us that these Native artists are participating in a larger global conversation and bring deeply informed views about stereotypes to the table. Rickard expresses a strongly held belief that exhibitions like *HIDE* are "integral keystones of the theoretical shift from deconstruction to reconstruction."

In the final chapter, Richard William Hill (Cree) asks us to enter a complicated conversation about the multiple layers of meaning articulated throughout the exhibition. He guides us through the history of representation, posing questions about what is authentic in Indian art, while at the same time recognizing that many of us are searching for authenticity in our lives and surroundings (authenticity being that particular quality many seek when looking at "real" Indian artifacts and art). This exhibition certainly compels us to look at not only the surface, but also the deeper history that informs it, including colonial racism. Hill instructs us about particular counterpoints and hierarchies such as nature versus culture, primitive versus civilized, heathen versus Christian. To really grasp this point, we need to look beyond the surface of the work to the details, and seek the undercurrent of its meaning.

While many contemporary artists of our era focus primarily on formal issues of expression, creating realistic depictions (portraits, landscapes, still lifes) or non-objective, abstract images (two-dimensional, 3-D, or works incorporating moving images), all of the artists featured in *HIDE* make art in order to deal with Big Issues. The undercurrent is about movement and action. For these particular contemporary Native artists, their choice of source materials and their creative inspiration comes from their tribal histories and identities. Indeed, their artistic practice can frequently be transgressive and cross many boundaries, whether cultural, geographic, tribal, or global. This is the quality and depth that make the featured work get under our skins and often deep into our hearts.

John Haworth (Cherokee)
Director, George Gustav Heye Center, National Museum of the American Indian

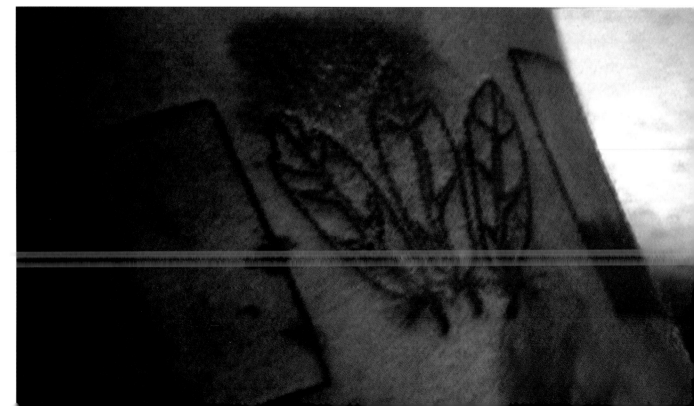

HIDE

By all the unwritten laws of savage warfare it is always the redskin who attacks, and with the wiliness of his race he does it just before the dawn, at which time he knows the courage of the whites to be at its lowest ebb.

J. M. Barrie, *Peter and Wendy* (1911)[1]

For Native people, skin encompasses an entire universe of meaning. Our own skin functions as a canvas that we can inscribe with messages about our identity, or use as a shield, protecting and hiding our secrets. Animal skin as a material, used for protection and artistic expression, also has a long history within Native culture. Whether considering hide or Native skin, skin is a deeply symbolic reminder of historical misrepresentation, exploitation, and racial politics. Native artists draw upon all of these sources to create compelling work that engages the intimate and communal. Rather than hide difficult issues, they expose what is beneath the surface. Like the material itself, their work is visceral and tactile. They tackle the thorny topics of stereotypes and blood quantum and explore personal issues such as scars or secrets. In their challenging work, Native artists interrupt our understanding of race, distort our perception of "skin," and violate the artificial boundaries created by this potent subject matter.

Since the earliest contact with Native people of the Americas, the Native body has been a source of fascination. Artists, anthropologists, explorers, and curious readers have all been enraptured, titillated, and obsessed with the sight of Native Americans with and without clothing. Early European explorers, as reflected in their journals and accounts, were enthralled with the relative nakedness of Native people, particularly in the places where contact first occurred. As Native people began to adopt European-style dress, non-Native society fixated on an imagined visual paradigm of Indian authenticity that consisted of long hair, hide clothing, and dark, exposed skin. These external and cultural attributes were believed to express essential Native characteristics such as savagery or closeness to nature. In the twentieth century, popular images of hide tipis, moccasins, bare-chested braves

Sioux buffalo robe (detail), ca. 1850. Buffalo hide and paint, 268 x 215 cm. 02/5354.

Nadia Myre, *Inkanatatation*, 2004. Digital video still. Collection of the artist. Art © Nadia Myre/Licensed by CARCC, Ontario and VAGA, New York.

and buckskin-adorned women in the early silent films, sports mascots, and images in mass-marketing cemented these associations. Stereotypes about Indian identity and debates about authenticity associated with skin and blood continue to shadow Native people both within their own communities and in the larger world.

Skin is also a material with complex associations for Native people. Historically, animal skin and hide are recognizable as prototypical Native materials alongside beads and feathers. As a medium, it has been used by Native people for centuries for its flexibility and durability. As a surface, it has served as a canvas for telling stories or recording histories in paint, quillwork, and beads, in addition to having been used to create protective barriers from the elements. Worn as clothing or stretched and formed into structures such as boxes or hide lodges, animal skin is ubiquitous in Native material culture throughout the Americas. This cultural and artistic use of hide and skin extends deep into history. Its perishable nature, however, makes some of the oldest examples of the media difficult to trace; the great majority of skin objects served regular functions and were designed to deteriorate through use over time.

Even the word itself—"skin" or "skins"—regardless of its casual usage among some Native people, still has the potential to touch a nerve. For some, it evokes the term "redskins" and all of its derogatory associations, particularly the cartooning of Native people for commercial uses such as sports mascots; for others it is a less-loaded, insider slang.[2] Ironically, research by linguist Ives Goddard has revealed the origin of the term "redskins" as self-referential, used in early nineteenth-century public remarks and speeches by Native leaders such as Meskwaki Chief Black Thunder and Omaha Chief Big Elk. Based on the eighteenth-century common use of the terms "red" and "white" as racial designations, Goddard proposes that the use of "redskins" by Native leaders to refer to Native people collectively (rather than as individual tribes or nations) was adopted to affirm solidarity and express a growing sense of pan-Indian identity. Goddard further suggests that it was the popularity of James Fenimore Cooper's novels, including *The Pioneers* (1823) and *The Last of the Mohicans* (1826), which led to the widespread adoption of the term as a common colloquialism, largely removed from direct exchange with Native people.[3]

By the twentieth century, the pejorative use of "redskins" paired with derogatory imagery led to the negative associations many Native people have with the term today. The stubborn resistance of professional and collegiate sports entities to bring an end to the outdated and offensive use of Indian caricature further imbeds these negative, combative associations. Although in 2007 the mascot "Chief Illiniwek" of the University of Illinois was finally retired after years of protest and public pressure, the image "Chief Wahoo" of the Cleveland Indians baseball team persists as a commercial trademark.[4] Over the past twenty years, several Native activists have taken it upon themselves to draw attention to the misuse and stereotyping of American Indians in the sports community through public protests, picketing of sports events, letter writing, debates in the media, and even lawsuits.[5]

The issue, at its core, is the misrepresentation of Native people. Reducing a culture to a simplistic reference to skin color ("redskins") or visual shorthand (mascot imag-

Jason Lujan, *Indian Interpolations I (Ghost Dog)*, 2004. Digital video still.

ery) dehumanizes generations of complex and diverse peoples. Numerous Native artists have taken an interventionist approach to the subject, engaging the imagery as a way to subvert the stereotype. Two significant examples of this approach include the billboard *Smile for Racism* (1996) by Edgar Heap of Birds (Cheyenne/Arapaho, b. 1954), which transformed a Chief Wahoo–type cartoon into a demonic image, and more recently, the series *Indian Interpolations I* (2004) *and II* (2006) by Jason Lujan (Apache, b. 1971). For *Indian Interpolations I*, Lujan downloaded copies of commercially released films featuring Native actors and intermittently superimposed commercial Native American imagery, such as Chief Wahoo, over their faces. According to the artist, he did this in order "to interrupt the flow of the visual narrative and draw attention to the commercialization of 'playing Indian.'" Lujan's intent is to "interrupt the movie's image of the Indian" with his "own political perception of media representation of Indians, for a brief moment."[6] Heap of Birds's and Lujan's interventions enlist public and commercial space to create a dialogue with unwitting consumers. Lujan's work, in particular, is a type of "culture jamming" or interruption of a commercial message that law professor Sonia Katyal has described as "semiotic disobedience," in which the artist has taken a commercial symbol, ascribed it with a new meaning, and shifted it "into an expression of political significance."[7]

Physical representation is a potent subject for Native Americans, particularly because of the historical mistreatment of the Native body, both living and dead. While European philosophers and scientists debated the humanity and perceived inferiority of Native people in the seventeenth and eighteenth centuries, the physical remains of Native people were treated disrespectfully by colonists, the military, and the scientific community.[8] Human remains collected as trophies, bounties, or specimens for study often ended up in museum collections established in the United States and Europe during the nineteenth century. Native people have even been collected as living anthropological specimens, such as Ishi, a Yahi survivor of the

California Indian genocide and one of the best-known cases of a Native American who was given a home in an anthropology museum (now the Phoebe A. Hearst Museum of Anthropology at the University of California, Berkeley). He lived in the museum, demonstrating his culture to the public from 1911 until his death in 1916 when, against his stated wishes, he was autopsied and his brain was transferred to the Smithsonian Institution for study.[9] There were other, similar cases such as that of Quisuk, who, with a small group of other Inuit, was brought from Greenland in 1897 to New York City's American Museum of Natural History by the explorer and anthropologist Robert Peary and died of infectious disease shortly thereafter. The only survivor of the group, his son Minik, protested the subsequent display of his father's skeleton at the museum and demanded that it and the remains of his other community members be removed for a proper burial. Remarkably, the remains of Quisuk and the three other Inuit in the party were not repatriated to Greenland until the early 1990s. Ishi's brain was repatriated by the Smithsonian's National Museum of Natural History in 2000.[10]

The exhibition of contemporary human remains outside an explicitly medical setting continues to have an aura of taboo. Recent exhibitions of preserved cadavers, with the skin completely or partially removed, have attracted controversy despite their promotion as educational experiences. Although they attract large audiences, *Bodies Revealed* and *Bodies . . . The Exhibition* raise concerns about the origins of the "specimens" and the ethics of displaying human remains publicly.[11] With the cadaver's identity erased, some critics have been concerned that audiences might forget they are looking at a real person. As educator Elaine Catz, who resigned from Pittsburgh's Carnegie Science Center in protest over the museum's plans to host *Bodies* in 2007, explained, "When we dehumanize the dead, it becomes easier to dehumanize the living."[12] The core of the ethical argument, however, has been about consent, a concern that is also at the heart of the dispute over the treatment of Native American human remains in museum collections.[13]

Since the passing of the Native American Graves Protection and Repatriation Act (NAGPRA), enacted in 1990 to ensure the respectful disposition of Native American human remains and sacred objects by museums, many human remains have been and continue to be returned to tribes for reburial; yet the symbolic impact of centuries-old collecting practices is deep. Native American artists have addressed the objectification of the Native body as anthropological specimens in numerous ways over the last twenty-five years, the most memorable examples being in performance works such as *The Artifact Piece*, first performed by James Luna (Luiseño, b. 1950) in 1987 and *Artifact #671B* by Rebecca Belmore (Anishinaabe, b. 1960), performed in 1988. In both works, the artists literally enacted the role of a museum specimen by performing as a passive object on display (Luna) or in storage (Belmore). By positioning themselves as artifacts, they became symbolic of the generations of Native people whose remains were collected, displayed, and stored on museum shelves like so many other artifacts from dead cultures. Many Native artists like Luna and

Hide Painting

Hide as a surface for creative expression holds an important place in Native culture. However, its universal use—from clothing to decorated pouch to storyboard canvas—is ironically matched by its perishable nature. Historically, the great majority of skin objects served specific regular functions and, because they were of an organic nature, were destined to be consumed through use over time. Their limited preservation does not reflect the deep history of hide paintings as a significant portable and malleable art form.

Sioux buffalo robe, ca. 1850. Buffalo hide and paint, 268 x 215 cm. 02/5354.

Just as the use of animal skin is ubiquitous in Native culture, there exists a respect for the animal and a noted effort to carefully utilize its resources and materials; the bond is close between human beings and the animals on which they depend for survival. In general, simple observances that maintained respectful practices within hide artwork included no wanton killing, careful butchering (often following prescribed guidelines), and attentive disposal of the carcass and any remaining bones so that dogs could not debase them.

The sunburst (also called "war bonnet") design of this particular Sioux buffalo-hide robe mimics the symmetrical, geometric designs found on other hide objects and art forms. It contrasts significantly with the figure-strewn, narrative story lines of other hide-based work such as winter counts, but it resembles parfleche and hide clothing decoration in its clarity and boldness.

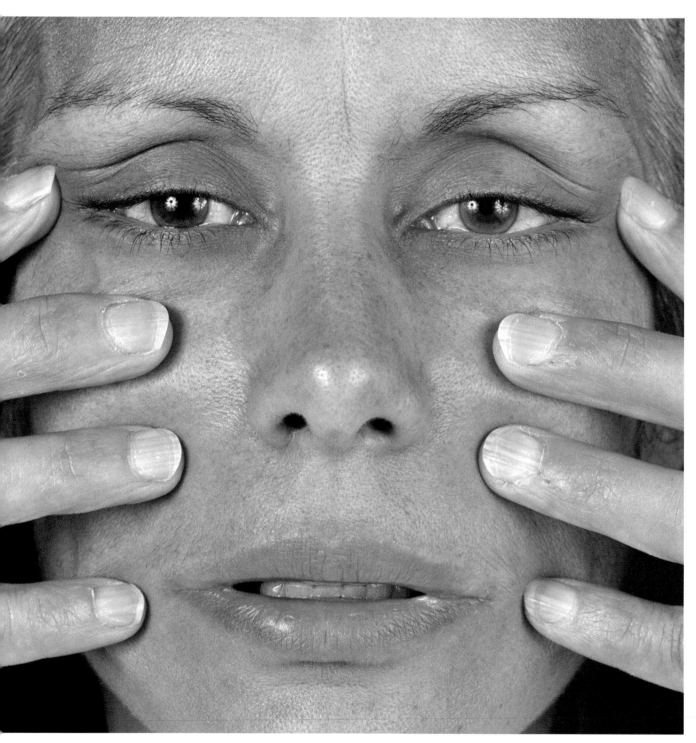

Arthur Renwick, *Jani*, 2006. Digital
print (artist's proof 2, ed. of 3), 119.4
x 114.3 cm. Collection of the artist.

Erica Lord, *I Tan to Look More Native*, 2006. Digital print, 10.2 x 12.7 cm.

Rebecca Belmore, *Fringe*, 2008. Transparency in lightbox, 243.8 x 16.5 x 81.3 cm.

Belmore have shifted the voice and the subject, often utilizing their own bodies and skin as both the medium and the message.

Several artists use different methods to scar their skin temporarily or permanently to create their arresting imagery. For the photographic series *The Tanning Project* (2005), Erica Lord (Athabascan/Inupiat, b. 1978) incorporated the photographic technique known as dodging and burning, using her skin as the paper and a tanning booth to darken her skin around several different phrases: "I Tan to Look More Native" across her back, "Indian Looking" down one arm, and "Half-Breed" across her chest. She chose phrases that confront the insecurities and superficial characteristics that both non-Native and Native people use to assess mixed-race Indians. Using her body to symbolize Indian land and culture, she goes even further in her provocation by burning in the phrase "Colonize Me" down her leg; photographed in a kneeling pose that emphasizes her nudity, she is exposed as both sexually vulnerable and receptive. In this instance, her body becomes a metaphor for the land.

The personification of the earth as female, a living entity that sustains life, is common in Native belief systems, so it is not surprising that many artists have used the Native body symbolically or literally to represent the land. Just as the skin protects the body, the surface of the earth is also a protective covering. Rebecca Belmore uses the body of a Native woman to symbolize the rape of the land by the colonizer in her recent photographic work, *Fringe* (2008). In it, the woman lies facing away from the camera, retaining a degree of anonymity and mystery, while her thin, exposed right arm and her protruding shoulder blades suggest hardship and maybe hunger. Her bare back is exposed to reveal a deep and gory gash, roughly stitched together with loose threads that appear to be sinew. Strings of red beads drip down like blood in irregular lines that remind the viewer of feathers or decorative fringe. A thick

scar is forming beneath this brutal wound, and the stitching appears as an attempt at repair and maybe even a measure of reconciliation. The imagery is compelling as a metaphor for the earth, but is also likely meant to comment on the ongoing violence against women in Native communities. These are wounds that continue to be reopened and seem to never heal.

Skin, whether human, animal, or artificial, is at once a simple and complex material. Its surface is both fragile and deceptively strong, revealing injuries, age, and experience. As a membrane that separates the inside of the body from the outside world, it acts as a boundary or threshold between the interior and the exterior. The artists selected for *HIDE* draw upon this rich subject and material in multifaceted ways, using both the substance and concept of skin as metaphors for widespread issues surrounding race and representation, as well as personal and historical trauma and perseverance. Sonya Kelliher-Combs, Nadia Myre, and Michael Belmore each present bodies of sculptural and mixed-media work that explore skin as a surface, revealing, concealing, and defining. The vision of these artists awakens the senses, drawing the audience into a tactile experience of the materiality of their work as well as making them think about the complex ideas that emerge from this compelling art. The photographers invited to participate in the exhibition—Arthur Renwick, KC Adams, Terrance Houle, Rosalie Favell, and Sarah Sense—have created images of Native people in a diverse collection of portraits that play with and challenge our notions about the representation of Native people. Together, they address the many complexities of skin as both a material and a metaphor.

Skin(s)

The construction and identification of corporeal forms is mediated by the crucial work of skin—as both biological tissue and discursive schema overdetermined by colonialism's obsession with racial and species categorizations. As skin molds itself around bodily contours, it both covers over and yet also throws into relief the real and imagined anatomies beneath the surface.

Pauline Wakeham, *Taxidermic Signs: Reconstructing Aboriginality* (2008)[14]

Sonya Kelliher-Combs creates compelling and sophisticated sculptural and mixed-media work that captures both vulnerability and strength in its organic and synthetic materials. The only artist in the exhibition who incorporates animal hides and viscera into her art, she creates semi-transparent and opaque skins and ambiguous forms that are intriguing, inviting, and sometimes discomforting. A repeating motif in her work, the amorphous pouch form, addresses containment and concealment. In the installation *Common Thread* (2008–10), these repeating forms are strung together on the wall, each with its own individual shape, color, and personality. Constructed with reindeer and sheep rawhide, they have an eerie, taxidermic quality that is familiar yet foreign. As Pauline Wakeham discusses in her analysis of the semiotics of taxidermy and the preservation of Native culture in museum displays, preserved flesh is coded with death and decay and represents a

Sonya Kelliher-Combs, *Common Thread*, 2008–10. Reindeer and sheep rawhide, nylon thread, variable dimensions. Collection of the artist.

fetishizing of figures of extinction.[15] Kelliher-Combs's enigmatic pouches appear to have covered some forms that have now vanished, leaving them as ghostly, empty shells. As sculptural forms, they are perfect containers for the artist to wrestle with secrets that are unspeakable or forced into hiding.

The series *Brand* (2009, p. 24) is also a layered, mixed-media work that draws together a wide variety of animal hides and gut products such as walrus stomach; seal intestine; reindeer, polar bear, elk, and moose fur; seal and sea lion skin; reindeer rawhide; and pig intestine as well as other organic (human hair, paper, cotton cloth) and inorganic (acrylic polymer, nylon thread) materials. The work, consisting of a suite of fifteen panels, is an exploration of stretched skin as a surface—marked, manipulated, deformed, or left bare. She abuses these skins, stitching, shaving, and branding them, and attaches them with grommets and beads. A circular shape, which she refers to as a pore, recurs on each work, sometimes as an image and other times as an actual opening or passage. For Kelliher-Combs, this work is about "making things our own, ownership and control," as she manipulates these primarily natural materials by stretching them into very unnatural shapes over rectangular frames.[16]

Although she has been lauded for her use of traditional Native Alaskan materials, especially those derived from sea mammals, Kelliher-Combs has not been deterred by their physical limitations. It was clear to her, after early experiments stretching walrus gut onto frames, that she needed a more flexible and forgiving material. Instead, she began to work with acrylic polymer to build artificial skins that could act as complex canvases. In addition to adhering materials to these surfaces, she began to infuse them with color and imbed materials such as hair and thread within the layers. The pouch form emerged as a recurring motif, now in silhouette, cut from flattened pieces of walrus stomach and captured in the layers of synthetic media.

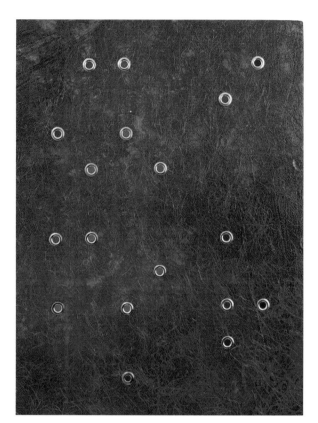

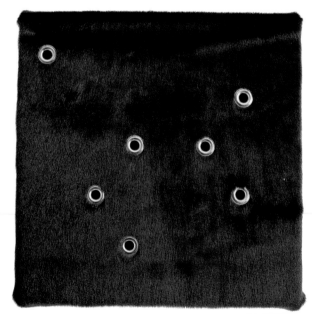

(Clockwise, from above) Sonya Kelliher-Combs, *Sea Lion Brand with Blue*, 2009. Sea lion skin/fur with nylon thread, 61 x 76.2 cm; *Red Reindeer Brand*, 2009. Reindeer fur, acrylic polymer, cotton fabric and metal grommets, 61 x 45.7 cm; *Black Seal Brand*, 2009. Dyed seal skin with metal grommets, 25.4 x 25.4 cm. Collection of the artist.

Sonya Kelliher-Combs, *Fern Walrus Family Portrait*, 2008. Acrylic polymer, nylon thread, paper, and walrus stomach, 61 x 61 cm. Collection of Donna Goldsmith and John Letourneau.

Using the transparency of these artificial skins, Kelliher-Combs is also able to harness light and shadow. The continuing series, *Walrus Family Portraits*, demonstrates her use of this evolving process to dramatic effect. In the recent work, embedded hairs emerge from the picture plane, hanging down or clustering in tufts like the trim on a parka.

A subtle, minimalist installation, *Shedding Skin* (2010) is a large-scale, meditative work on lineage and relationships. It is composed of over four thousand sewing needles embedded in both sides of a free standing wall and laced through with flesh-colored thread. Each of the threads wraps around the wall, outlines the familiar pouch or tusk form, and falls into a soft heap on the platform below. Viewers follow the lines of each thread, some of which break and restart, while others are continu-

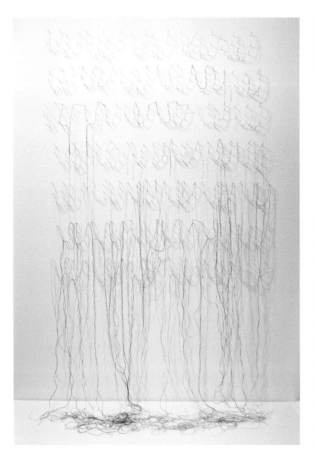

Sonya Kelliher-Combs, *Shedding Skin*, 2010. Needles, nylon and cotton thread, variable dimensions. Collection of the artist.

ous. Kelliher-Combs envisions these lines as metaphors for lineage and the passage of time; some continue to the end, while other relationships and connections are broken. As in *Common Thread*, the lines each have their own individual history and path but together form a type of collective or community. A secondary composition is the shadow cast on the wall beneath the threads, which creates a temporary imprint. The installation itself is temporal and is as much about the act of sewing as it is about the finished form. Despite the artist's use of cotton thread instead of animal products, the title, as well as the needles and flesh-colored thread, gives the work a whiff of the macabre.

Nadia Myre's work also has a visceral edge. Her short video, *Inkanatatation* (2004, p. 14) is a gripping record of the artist being tattooed with an image of an indigenous flag for Canada, designed by Mohawk artist Greg Hill (b. 1967). Based on the Canadian national flag's central maple leaf, the design here has been replaced by three feathers to represent the three major indigenous groups in Canada: First Nations, Métis, and Inuit. In this silent work, we are repeatedly brought back to her arm as it is being tattooed with red ink. Tattooing can be uncomfortable to watch; it is a controlled but violent and sometimes bloody act. In this instance, the blood seems to be copious since we cannot distinguish between it and the red ink. Despite the implied pain, the act of having this image tattooed on her skin is an empowering and deliberate act that expresses her indigeneity. This act of tattooing, as the title implies (*Kanata* is a Mohawk word meaning "town" or "settlement"), is not about ornamentation but has an affinity with ritual tattooing.

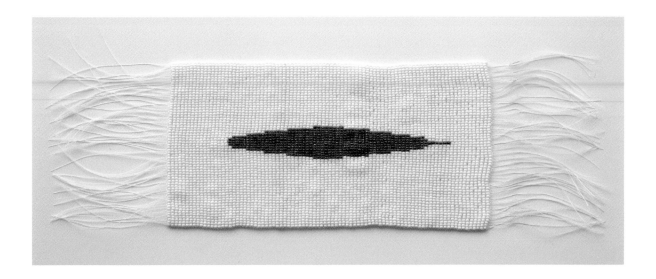

Nadia Myre, *Scarscapes* (detail), 2009. Glass beads, cotton thread, 35.6 x 10.2 cm each. Collection of the artist.

Like Kelliher-Combs, Nadia Myre's imparts a haptic, personal quality to her art along with a focus on repetition. Myre's epic work known as *The Scar Project* (2005–ongoing, p. 55) contains hundreds of ripped, sewn, and shaped canvases, each of which tells an individual story. Initiated as a personal exploration of her scars, the project grew into a cooperative endeavor, using workshops to enlist numerous individuals to write their personal scar stories and create their own scar canvases as a contribution to the project. The scars could be psychological or physical wounds that still hurt or were healed; like literal scars, the healing process sometimes makes you stronger. The canvases, which now number over five hundred, have become a series of sculptural reliefs that she uses to create large installations, often including the collected stories themselves. As she brings this project to a close, she has started to examine the collected imagery and reflect upon images that repeat throughout the series. *Scarscapes* (2009), a series of five loom-woven beaded works, examines the motifs of pain and survival. These images, like the scars themselves, have multiple meanings. The stitched scar, for example, shows the hands of a healer or could be interpreted as a ladder or bridge.

While both Kelliher-Combs and Myre use organic and artificial materials that mimic the texture and malleability of natural skin, Michael Belmore chose a markedly different route. Belmore uses sculpted river stones and hammered copper to explore the surface of the earth. Even though his art degree concentration was in plastics, he has moved from the manipulation of synthetics to the arduous process of using natural and essential materials. His sculptural work with stone is subtle, and has at times verged toward earthwork, or art that is both from and of the landscape. Belmore's previous stone sculpture utilized traditional Western approaches to the media; a series, *Grotesques of the Eastern Woodlands* (2005), for example, included gargoyle-like figures, and more recently, he created relief depictions of Misshipeshu, the Ojibwe underwater lynx (*Colony*, 2007).[17] With *Upland* (2005), a permanent sculptural installation within the landscape 71 miles north of Toronto, he began however to take a minimalist approach to his materials. At first glance,

Michael Belmore, *Upland*, 2005.
Stone installation, Ontario.

Upland seems to be only a collection of river rocks randomly strewn in a gully. Closer examination reveals that these smooth rocks are nested together, overlapping in unnatural configurations as if they have melded together to create a bubbling surface.[18] In Belmore's subsequent work with stones, he has concentrated less on the absolute form of each rock and more on the relationships between them, where their surfaces—ground smooth by the artist—meet. The worked surfaces in *Flux* (2010), a sculptural installation presented in this exhibition, have been coated with a thin skin of gold leaf, which subtly reflects light at each of the stone junctures.

Belmore's monumental recent work in hammered and chiseled copper explores the surface of the land using a more direct and sensual approach. Utilizing three-by-seven-foot sheets of copper, Belmore has created meditative reflections on the North American topography—land and water—that surrounds and sustains us. These environmental skins are a type of "earth mapping" that philosopher and theorist Edward S. Casey has described as reflecting a nuanced and essential understanding of the land: "The core of this coherence is not that of being a representation of land (or sea) in the ordinary delimited meanings of *representation* (pictorial, isomorphic, etc.) but that of being a *re-presentation* of the earth, its *re-implacement* in an artwork, its *relocation* there."[19] These works, including both *Origins* (2009, p. 74) and *Dark Water* (2009–10, pp. 66, 75, 77) transform heavy, inert metal sheets into thin, undulating membranes with channels that ebb and flow, swelling and receding in organic waves as if they are concealing and restraining a tremendous force beneath the surface. Like any skin, its surface shows the scars, whether from human activity and manipulation or natural events and processes such as wind and rain erosion or geologic events. Careful examination also reveals human environmental impact where hard and unyielding architectural docks interrupt the organic and fluid natural shorelines.

Showing Skin

The literal depiction of Indian skin through photography has a long and storied history, from the romantic turn-of-the-twentieth-century photogravures by Edward Curtis and documentary images by early anthropologists and ethnographers to the diverse and sometimes confrontational work of Native photographers in the twentieth century. Native photographers have been featured in several exhibitions and publications that, in many cases, underscore their self-conscious awareness of the tropes of Indian representation as each photographer takes control of the image.[20] In the 1980s and '90s, many sought to picture Native communities from the inside—as they are, not as they are expected to be—while others produced those that were overtly political in nature. The photographers chosen for *HIDE* have constructed powerful portraits of themselves and their personal communities, building images that are intimate and subtly subversive and, as Jolene Rickard describes in her essay in this book, that form "a collective deconstruction of the representation of indigenous peoples."

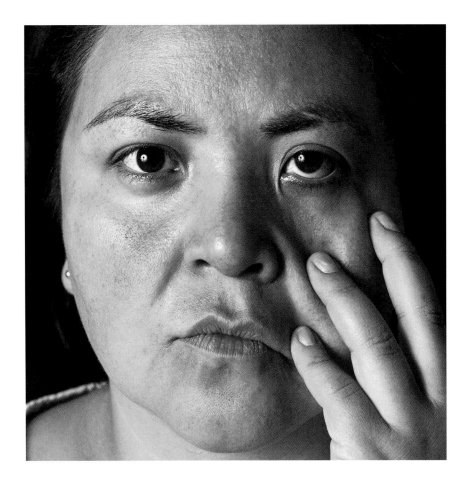

Arthur Renwick, *Eden*, 2006. Digital print (artist's proof, ed. of 3), 119.4 x 114.3 cm; (below) *Fernando*, 2006. Digital print (ed. 3/3), 119.4 x 114.3 cm. Collection of the artist.

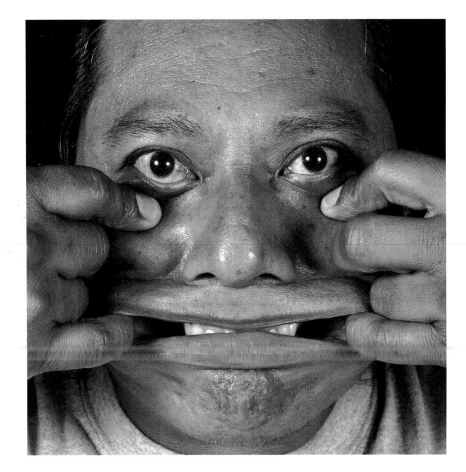

ORLAN, *Refiguration: Self-Hybrid-ization, American Indian Series no. 7,* portrait painting of Tís-se-wóo-na-tís, She Who Bathes Her Knees, Wife Of The Chief, with ORLAN's photographic portrait, 2005. Digital photograph, 152.4 x 124.4 cm.

The series *Mask* (2006) is a collection of powerful portraits by Toronto-based photographer Arthur Renwick. He is primarily known for his landscape photography and has rarely focused his lens on people, let alone to create portraits. The impetus for this series involved his personal reflections upon historical depictions of Native people: the romanticism, the sepia tones, and the soft focus on the "vanishing race." Before taking the portraits of models drawn from the Native community of artists, writers, and performers in the Toronto area, he asked the subjects to first consider how Native people are portrayed in photography and then decide how they wanted to be seen. Remarkably, each model independently chose to alter his or her own face when confronting the camera by stretching, squeezing, and distorting skin. The result is that their faces begin to appear quite literally as masks.

This confrontational series, which Renwick prints in a large, forty-six-by-forty-four-inch format, is not beautiful and romantic but visceral and inescapable. Closely cropped, the images appear in a large scale, with each pore, hair, and broken blood vessel there for all to see. The series recalls the work of the French artist ORLAN (b. 1947), who used the skin of her own face as a malleable surface on which to create her art through surgery. ORLAN has described her face as only a mask; the surgical alterations are her performance. Art historian C. Jill O'Bryan writes about the mask that is not "superficial": "Although the mask is generally an object that can be worn or removed at will, it invests a complex register of identity; it conceals one identity at the same time that it reveals another."[21] Using this assessment, then it is clear that the masks Renwick's models have chosen to "wear" for these portraits are ones that express both humor and hostility, and most plainly, a desire to be seen.

At the other end of the spectrum is the work of Métis artist KC Adams and her ongoing series *Cyborg Hybrids*. Like Renwick, Adams draws her models from the indigenous arts community, primarily focusing on visual and performing artists, both contemporary and traditional, and art curators. Drawing on Donna Haraway's 1985 "Cyborg Manifesto," which describes a cyborg as a "cybernetic organism, a hybrid of machine and organism, a creature of social reality as well as a creature of fiction," Adams's portraits are of people who are racial hybrids with both Native and European ancestry. Each participant is someone who also incorporates technology in his or her daily life, such as by utilizing computers or the Internet (perhaps it would be a greater challenge to find someone who is not intimately intertwined with technology). Haraway's manifesto sought to break away from patriarchal notions of capital, gender, sexuality, and the binaries of human/machine, good/evil, and fear/fascination by creating a world of humans that had fully merged with machines.[22]

Adams strives to create these ideal cyborgs in her work by directly addressing race and representation.

Adams's models are dressed in white, with a white background. The environment touches upon widely held associations with the color white, including purity, cleanliness, and goodness. The models all wear bone chokers to reference their indigeneity, which curator Ryan Rice has identified as a "'branding strategy,' a signifier of inheritance and unity, and an indicator of a growing society."[23] The artist has scrubbed their faces of wrinkles, blemishes, and other imperfections, and given their skin a uniform and glowing bronze hue. Like Renwick, she also has a conversation with her models during their photo sessions, discussing how their experience living as racial hybrids may have influenced their perception by others. Their stories are reflected in the words beaded upon their shirts. In the new series, *Cyborg Hybrids—New York* (2009), the phrase "My Grandmother Was Cherokee" is beaded across the chest of the subject Tom (p. 34), a dancer and choreographer. The cliché of the suspected "white imposter" is this New York Native's reality. Though he has a fair complexion, both of his grandmothers were, in fact, Cherokee. *Cyborg Hybrid* Yatika, a visual artist living in Brooklyn, has also spent many years as a bike messenger. Clients at his regular stops do not know his name, they just call him "Chief." The phrase "Adopted Out" on *Cyborg Hybrid* Donna's shirt reminds us of the complex personal histories that contemporary Native people negotiate in asserting

Rosalie Favell, *Ryan Rice*, 2008.
From the *Facing the Camera* series,
digital print, 61 x 50.8 cm. Collection
of the artist.

their right to Native identity. In each of these portraits Adams subversively confronts the audience; she draws them in with glamorous, otherworldly images, dares them to face the stereotypes that continue to dog contemporary Native people, and then challenges all of our ideas about authenticity.

Rosalie Favell's series *Facing the Camera* (2008–present) offers yet another approach. Like Renwick and Adams, she also draws her subjects from the indigenous community of artists and curators, but there is also an implicit desire to create wholeness in this series. Each of her subjects is named in full, so we know exactly who we are seeing in her portraits. Ryan Rice is pictured with his full name in Favell's image, whereas *Cyborg Hybrid Ryan* (2007), an earlier portrait by Adams, is a bit mysterious if you do not know Rice or are only familiar with his work as an artist and curator. Renwick and Adams have created work about their community, but it retains a private and privileged reading; the models also retain a degree of

KC Adams, *Cyborg Hybrid Tom*, 2009.
Digital print, 50.8 x 35.6 cm. Collection
of the artist.

Virtual Skins

The term "skin" has many meanings and applications in cyberspace. In hardware, it's a covering, like choosing a pink case for your laptop. In software, it is the illusion of surface in computer environments. Within programs that create virtual realities, skins are images wrapped onto 3-D models, like a picture of bark wrapped around a cylinder to make it seem like a tree, or the illusion of human skin (including eyes, nose, etc.) that makes an avatar look more realistic.

Skawennati (b. 1969), a Mohawk artist, writer, and independent curator, has staked a claim in cyberspace with the creation of AbTeC (Aboriginal Territories in Cyberspace) in collaboration with artist Jason E. Lewis. A network of artists and computer specialists, AbTeC seeks to define and determine Native presence with technology. The headquarters of this initiative, AbTeC Island, is a virtual environment within the multiplayer online game *Second Life* where members are constructing environments and avatars in an effort to encourage Native cultural expression within this new platform. Projects include "Skins: Storytelling in Cyberspace," a "modding" (slang for modifying content to be shared on the web) workshop for Native youth (which, in addition to preserving and promoting cultural knowledge, teaches skills usable in the growing video game industry to encourage youth to be producers and not just consumers of these technologies); a "machinima" (the use of real-world filmmaking techniques in a virtual environment) series called *TimeTraveller* starring Hunter (pictured above), an angry young Mohawk man from the twenty-second century; and an art gallery filled with digital installations that could only be experienced in *Second Life*.

Skawennati, *TimeTraveller*, 2008. Production still. Hunter hovers in front of the storage locker he calls home. *TimeTraveller* is being produced with the support of Aboriginal Territories in Cyberspace (www.AbTeC.org).

anonymity. Thomas King is well known as an acclaimed author and politician, but his "mask" is quite coy as he peeks out from behind his hand in Renwick's portrait (p. 121). Uncovering the layers of individual identity requires a bit of detective work for the viewer, and keeps control of the reading in the hands of both photographer *and* subject. Favell's *Facing the Camera* presents its subjects directly to the viewer. The photographer has captured each person in a relaxed and familiar manner; these are friends and respected colleagues. Most are dressed casually and comfortably. The black-and-white format is quite traditional in presentation but asks us to consider whether its very conventionality is revolutionary simply because it is so.

Terrance Houle and Sarah Sense are much more autobiographical in their compositions. Houle is known primarily in the indigenous arts community as a performance artist, although he has created memorable, humorous, and piquant work in collaboration with photographer Jarusha Brown. In these images, which often serve as documentary stages for what are essentially performative tableaux, Houle is the art director, actor, and protagonist. The *Urban Indian Series* (2007) serves as a narrative work that walks us through a "normal" day for an urban Indian, from morning until night, invisibly following him as he carries out his quotidian tasks: he picks out his clothes, kisses the lovely spouse goodbye, commutes to work, marks time in his office cubicle, eats lunch at a diner, drops by the music store to pick up some tunes, and even visits the grocery store before ending his day with a relaxing bath. The anomaly confronting us in this visual storyline is the urban setting juxtaposed with the subject's unexpected attire, which consists of traditional Grass Dance regalia, complete with ribbon and yarn fringe, and accompanied by beaded gauntlets and headband. The dissonance between what we expect and what we see creates a humorous response from most viewers. Historian Philip Deloria (Standing Rock Sioux) describes this dissonance as part of a widespread cultural phenomenon, indicative of Western culture's continuing rejection of the modernity of Native people: "Primitivism, technological incompetence, physical distance, and cultural difference—these have been the ways many Americans have imagined Indians . . . and such images have remained familiar currency in contemporary dealings with Native people."[24] Thus, Houle's imagery calls our attention to these assumptions, making the viewer laugh, and hopefully think.

In the video work *Metrosexual Indian* (2005), Houle attacks this issue from a different angle. As this short film opens, we meet the metrosexual Indian. He is an urbane fellow with a jaunty walk and hip city clothes. With a peppy music soundtrack in the background, he makes his rounds in town, chats on his cell phone, and even makes a mandatory stop to order a latte. Lurking in shadows, however, are three Indian thugs. They wear a hodgepodge of traditional signifiers, such as tourist-trap headdresses, and smoke cigarettes as they linger in a nearby alley. Eventually they confront him and a violent scuffle ensues. He is beaten for adopting white attributes, symbols, and technology—most notably his wristwatch. His embrace of contemporary culture clearly represents a challenge and threat to his reservation brothers who sternly put him in his place. In *Metrosexual Indian*, Houle engages the uncomfortable conflict

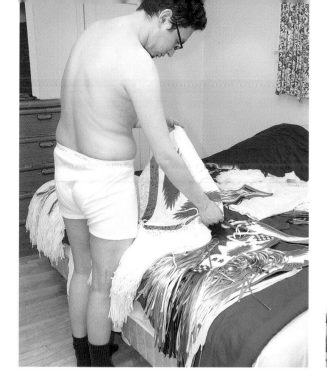

Terrance Houle, *Urban Indian Series* (nos. 1 & 2), 2007. Eight digital C-prints, 35.6 x 27.9 cm each. Collection of the artist. Photos by Jarusha Brown.

Terrance Houle, *Metrosexual Indian*, 2005. Publicity still.

Sarah Sense, *Karl 3* (detail), 2009.
Digital prints on paper and mylar,
artist tape, 121.9 x 243.8 cm.
Collection of the artist.

that haunts many Native people who live in urban environments: Native people themselves are also guilty of perpetuating stereotypes, pulling down other Indians who live outside reservation and cultural mores, and maintaining restrictive notions of what it means to be a contemporary Indian.

Sarah Sense creates a personal, familial portrait in her three-part photographic woven composition, *Karl* (2009). Sense has used herself as the subject in numerous works that combine pop-culture images of Indians. She not only sources Hollywood but has also incorporated turn-of-the-twentieth-century historic photos of famous Indians such as Sitting Bull and Geronimo into woven montages that include photos of herself in the various Indian guises. She has appeared as a child, dressed "Indian" in a small war bonnet by her mother, and as an adult self-consciously plays various stereotypical western roles dressed as characters such as the Indian maiden and cowgirl. Drawing on her Chitimacha heritage, Sense began weaving these disparate images into traditional basket forms; repeating patterns such as the "deer's eye" and "rabbit's paw" materialize throughout the baskets and mats. Complex images emerge from these earlier works, interleaving reality, fantasy, and tradition.

In *Karl*, Sense deepens the exploration, weaving together scraps of stories to create a personal narrative that incorporates the complexities of her family's histories. Like many Native artists, Sense comes from a family of mixed heritage. Her father's family is German, and both her father and grandfather—an aerospace engineer in the Cold War era—were named Karl Sense. Sense recently found copies of Karl Sense Sr.'s numerous published scientific papers as well as personal correspondences. A particular note struck her as it is laden with the unspoken tension between a father and son; reading between the lines, she found it both perfunctory and accusatory:

Karl, There are a couple of publications of mine that are missing. I can't find them.
Love, Dad

The first work in the series includes a photo of Karl Sr. wearing a lab coat as he works. The interwoven image is a composite of numbers and abstract formulas from his many publications as well as the text of the note to his son. In the second work, the note reappears, but the text is becoming obscure. An image of a child appears, as well as scientific drawings and a landscape from the Chitimacha reservation at sunset. The deconstruction and complexity increase in the third composition, which again includes the text of the note, another child, a likeness of the iconic John Wayne, and a self-portrait of Sarah atop a horse. The images become more and more fragmented as the works themselves become more incomplete. Although the first

Sarah Sense, *Karl 1*, 2009. Digital prints on paper and mylar, artist tape, 121.9 x 243.8 cm. Collection of the artist.

mat is woven completely, the second is missing about a third of the warps, and the third is woven only at the top. The loose fringe creates a willowy and less-concrete surface, evoking the transitory nature of these family stories and relationships as time passes.

The artists in *HIDE* demonstrate that skin continues to be a potent subject for Native people. The exhibition is both about appearances and more than appearances. It has only been a few decades since looking "Indian," in some circles, was considered to be a detriment to success and upward mobility. For others, selectively identifying as Indian presented greater opportunities. Being Indian, looking Indian, playing Indian—they are all about surface appearances, what they reveal, and what they hide. But they are also about what we choose to see. Many problems, conflicts, traumas, and biases are easier to ignore than to confront. The strength of this work lies not only in the technical mastery of the makers, but also in their bold exploration of uncomfortable subjects that are nevertheless very real and relevant to the contemporary experience. It is clear that the artists chosen for this exhibition do not want to hide from difficult issues but rather want to dig deeper with their work.

For Native artists, working on the surface is only the beginning.

Sonya Kelliher-Combs: Secret Skin

Few artists produce the kind of complex, densely layered, intimate art as Sonya Kelliher-Combs. In a sophisticated visual lexicon of biomorphic forms and shapes, Kelliher-Combs's art is quickly becoming some of the most discussed and sought out work by institutions and galleries, from a woman who has been on the art scene only since 1998. Of Inupiaq and Athabascan mixed heritage, a combination that informs her work, Kelliher-Combs is also enormously proud of her Irish and German roots and acknowledges that the diversity of her heritage is central to her identity as an artist, daughter, wife, and community member. In turn, her art is an integral part of her process of reclaiming a unique sense of self. She explains, "When it comes to my work, whether early or current, I have always considered it an extension of myself. Through painting, sculpture, and installation, I speak about identity."[1]

Kelliher-Combs's art is categorized as mixed-media painting, soft sculpture, collage, drawing, and installation. Her stylistic preference, however, is a pastiche of materials in primary shapes. Like the defined system of Northwest Coast formline design identified by artist and teacher Bill Holm, Kelliher-Combs has created a personal system of shapes, line, and forms that appear as ovoids or ellipses, parallel curved lines, swirling free-form graphic lines, and tight circles or rondelles.[2]

With almost obsessive energy, Kelliher-Combs incorporates her vocabulary into a repetitive process, creating several series of exhaustive, investigative works. One ongoing series is *Pores*, a reference to the circular holes or openings in hides or skin that permit passage between and among. Another is *Secrets*, which features an elliptical form constructed of gut or fur that can suggest male or female, container or portable pouch, and the retained or hidden. Pairs of "secret" forms appear in her ongoing mixed-media series *Walrus Family Portraits* as flat silhouettes, but also three-dimensionally in her sculpture and installations, such as *Common Thread* (2008–10, p. 23) and *Small Secrets* (2009).

Sonya Kelliher-Combs, *Salmon Walrus Family Portrait with Trim* (in progress), 2009–10. Acrylic polymer, walrus stomach, nylon thread, glass beads, archival ink, paper, fabric, and reindeer fur, 177.8 x 101.6 cm. Collection of the artist.

Sonya Kelliher-Combs, *Blue Pore
with Pink*, 2009. Acrylic polymer,
paper, and nylon thread, 62 x 62 cm.
Collection of the artist.

Sonya Kelliher-Combs, *Small Secrets*
(details), 2009. Walrus stomach,
human hair, glass beads, and nylon
thread, variable dimensions. Collection of the artist.

The pattern of multiple ivory tusks is a view familiar to hunters approaching marine mammals lounging in groups. The reference has another source as an appliqué motif found on clothing, however, including parkas worn in a family photograph of Kelliher-Combs's grandmother and great-uncle. In several works, Kelliher-Combs incorporates the signs and symbols drawn from sources learned while growing up in northern Alaska. She is never without these references; they appear in the repetition of the familiar and organic, yet are formulated in a style that is neither stereotype nor an overt reference to ethnicity. Kelliher-Combs addresses audiences in a visual language of older styles, patterns, and forms, yet transforms the dialogue through the manipulation of materials that extend and juxtapose what is expected with what is new.

Animal skin, both natural and synthetic, is the primary medium for most of Kelliher-Combs's art. Animal skin and hide once served multiple functions in all phases of human culture. In Kelliher-Combs's hands, skin's use is both symbolic and practical, becoming the canvas on which she inscribes a creative act. It is a natural surface, which Kelliher-Combs builds and uses to expose and obscure views of and into the work; she achieves this physical manipulation through layering, folding, scratching, and stretching the skin.

For Kelliher-Combs, skin stretched across the picture frame becomes a literal window that acts to mediate the process of self-examination with arrangements of shapes and layered objects. She describes the forms as metaphors, symbolic barriers that both keep out and retain personal and public knowledge and layers of meaning from a deeply personal vocabulary. Stretched or sewn-down animal membrane produces an opaqueness on the surface of the work that also obscures the artist's musings. Kelliher-Combs embeds other materials and objects, adding, scratching, and digging into the surface with additions of color that further obstruct the viewer's perspective, making it neither clear nor easily seen from any single direction. Although she permits us to look, she makes the view difficult and couched within an archaeological strata of texture, color, and form, forcing the viewer to consider other points of reference and perspectives.

Creating access or denying access is a subtle controlling act—a way to guard the private person—yet demonstrates a desire to reveal secrets, hidden just below the surface, to outsiders. It is a push/pull binary that seems to warn: Look, but not too closely; not all aspects of Native culture (or personal narrative) are accessible or intended for public knowledge. Kelliher-Combs explains, "In early works I addressed multicultural identity through the physical process of painting, layering images of human and animal forms to create expressionistic works communicating my relationship to the land, who I am, and where I come from. These ideas are still central in all aspects of my life and work."[3]

Through the membrane, Kelliher-Combs illuminates subjects that an audience might find problematic, such as abuse. "Many of the works . . . are difficult to make. Some I have spent years digesting before creation—in particular, those addressing issues like suicide and abuse. I do not know a single person who has not been

Mary Stotts Adams and Harry Brower Sr., Kelliher-Combs's grandmother and great-uncle, wearing parkas with tusk motif at neck, ca. 1940.

affected by either."⁴ Yet her desire to situate the art in galleries and museums reveals her deliberate intent to provide a channel toward openness. As secrets are exposed, the power of the unspoken is weakened. It is this objective that pushes forward the continuation of a serial body of work, produced since 2000, titled *Secrets*.

Kelliher-Combs, a woman aware of her role in the changing dynamic of Native people in communities that extend beyond northern Alaska, acknowledges that she is part of the growing group of cosmopolitan, formally educated, and well-traveled Natives who comprise the generation of children after the baby boom. Born in Bethel in 1969 and raised in Nome, Kelliher-Combs retains family ties to both her Native and Anglo heritages, the communities of her biological and adopted families. Living in Anchorage, she must continually travel from Alaska to the sites where international art is exhibited and sold in the Lower 48 and abroad.

Returning to Alaska after a recent residency in Southern California, the home-coming is, as always, a private moment to recover and assess what has changed, to recognize what has disappeared, and resume the routines with family and friends, the dynamics of a life that never slows. Commenting on her art and the intimate nature of the subjects she investigates, Kelliher-Combs observes: "My work is directly from personal experience; it's my interpretation, digested through me. It is an extension of myself. I can't speak for a whole community; I can only speak for myself."⁵ The

Sonya Kelliher-Combs, *Good-bye*, 2007. Historic collections installation from *Points of View VII: Con-Census*, Anchorage Museum at Rasmuson Center.

assessment of these experiences is an abstracted process that curator and art historian Julie Decker acknowledges in a discussion of her work, observing, "Kelliher-Combs seems less interested in mystery than she is in using her work as a process through which to examine her own present and past as well as those of her culture."[6]

In her recent gallery installations addressing social issues that Native art rarely examines or admits, the public reticence surrounding the secretive nature of abuse spurs Kelliher-Combs to openly challenge the subject, but with an understated delicacy so as not to overwhelm. An artist whose voice transcends the political dogma that reduces many discussions of Native art to rhetoric, Kelliher-Combs asks for consideration of subjects that are neither humorous nor convenient. She questions the real social dysfunction in small Native communities usually comprised of extended families; the demise of subsistence economies; the persistent presence of religious personnel in Native villages; related stories of child abuse; and suicide and its aftermath. Recognizing that she draws attention to secrets kept by several generations of abusers and that her agency may not be supported by everyone in Alaska's Native community, Kelliher-Combs observes, "Some embrace what I do, some do not."

Allison Kelliher and Sonya Kelliher-Combs preparing a walrus stomach, 1995.

Drawn from experiences growing up in Nome with summers in the country hunting and gathering, Kelliher-Combs wants her art to convey place, "the idea of where we are from, our different backgrounds," and connections that bring people together. If the connection is broken, as with Kelliher-Combs's loss of several relatives to suicide, the sense of loss is not only an emotional one but also becomes tangible as a visible element in her art. Much of her work retains a feeling of gravitas with an aura of public mourning that saturates each composition and recalls loss that can never be recovered.

Haunted, emotional, and tragic, several compositions become memorials that resound with a muted irony. A powerful example is *Goodbye*, featured in the exhibi-

Eva Hesse, *Tori*, 1969. Fiberglass on wire mesh. Largest of nine units 119.4 x 43.2 x 38.1 cm. Collection of the Philadelphia Museum of Art.

tion she curated in 2007 at the Anchorage Museum, *Points of View VII: Con-Census*. The installation of thirty-eight pairs of hide gloves and mittens honors Native people who committed suicide. Looking beyond her own family's losses, Kelliher-Combs acknowledges each life as part of a greater whole. Unlike an ethnographic exhibition of clothing, *Goodbye* is an assembly of intimate personal items, a recognition of how pervasive and all-encompassing loss can be in small, isolated communities.

While allowing dialogue to transpire by drawing attention to the issue, Kelliher-Combs struggles not to offend but rather to illuminate the suicide problem that is shared not only by Native communities, but all. Decker's discussion of Kelliher-Combs's art notes, "There is a sense of taboo associated with speaking about the issue in Native cultures. Kelliher-Combs does so in a way that symbolizes sorrow and loss in a more general sense, in an effort to speak to the perseverance of her cultures and to promote healing."[7] The struggle for Kelliher-Combs is in maintaining relationships with communities that are less about subsistence and more about the growth of an urban lifestyle in some ways at odds with both tradition and progress.

Kelliher-Combs's use of cast-off materials, the debris of communities, suggests an association with the minimalist works of Eva Hesse (1936–1970), whose use of remnants and industrial products altered the discussion of what constituted appropriate materials and added the notion of contained "ugliness" to aesthetic deliberation. Like Hesse, Kelliher-Combs both uses and emulates ordinary materials and cultural detritus in repetitive forms such as in *Common Thread* (2008–10). Using man-made fragments and animal viscera, stretched and reshaped across stretchers or sewn to fabric or skin, Kelliher-Combs leaves no doubt that not only is she using unconventional materials appropriately and ingeniously, but also that she is continuing the tradition of Native innovation and adaptation by adding new meaning and understanding to the study of American art.

Sonya Kelliher-Combs, *Judy's Secret Portrait*, 2008. Paper, beeswax, human hair, and nylon thread, 10.2 x 15.2 cm.

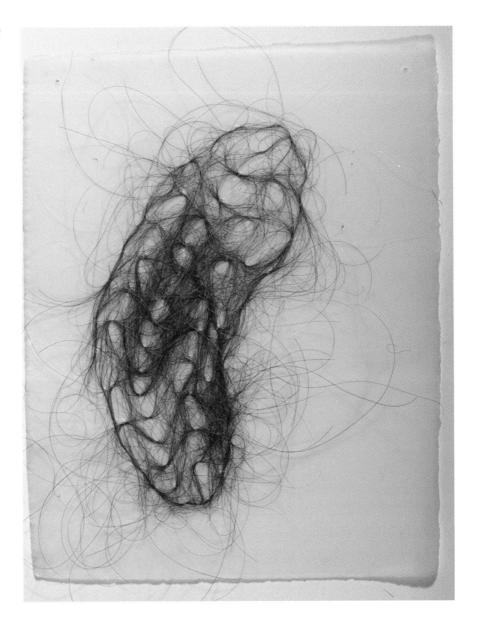

Although some may view her work as exclusively nontraditional arrangements in abstraction, it is connected to both contemporary and older forms of Alaska Native art, including sewing, tattooing, and ancient carving. The combinations of materials and oblique references to older traditions provide evidence of the inevitable change that is a powerful dynamic for Native cultures. Tradition must reflect change, and it is culture that mediates what is relevant and will continue. Without change, traditions and cultures cease and are forgotten. While some may decry this process and argue that "traditional" art is unchanging, such perspectives fail to acknowledge how creativity, by its very nature, is never frozen or arrested in some vague and nostalgic point in time. As anthropologist Bruce Bernstein points out, "Change is best understood in the context of Indian art as strength, because it produces a vibrancy that, in turn, creates survival."[8]

The focus on animal skin is a significant part of the Alaska Native heritage. In her work, Kelliher-Combs's use of hide and skin-like materials, natural and synthetic, is not limited to stretching and sewing; she gathers and affixes hide fragments bits and pieces of fabric remnants, human hair, offal such as walrus and seal intestine, polar bear and spotted seal fur, moose hide, and reindeer skin to larger works. She often constructs artificial skin from poured acrylic polymer, a process that adds layers and translucency as well. Drawings link with ancient hunting traditions of Alaska Natives, and Kelliher-Combs's use of a wide range of animal skins illustrates other concerns that challenge the idea of skin and hide as being exclusively utilitarian.

Although an organic allure emanates from her work, Kelliher-Combs's use of animal materials may seem contrary to an ecologically-aware "green" agenda. She clarifies this point, stating that she often purchases hides and gut from friends on remote St. Lawrence Island (a part of Alaska but closer to Russia in the Bering Strait) who rely on seasonal subsistence hunting. Typical materials in her mixed-media pieces, such as *Pores*, can include polar bear fur and hide, walrus and spotted seal intestine, whale pericardium, porcupine quill, moose hide, and human hair. Coupled with man-made debris and found remnants, she also includes glass trade beads, steel needles and straight pins, delicate fabric from women's undergarments, as well as a *kuspuk*, the fabric outer dress worn by Alaska Native women. With unlikely combinations that remain unconventional, Kelliher-Combs's art possesses a seductiveness that can simultaneously entice and repel.

The beauty of the translucent skin is an unexpected aesthetic. The stretched material explores, beyond the relationship to the natural world, a process of transformation where viscera is shaped, stretched, and altered. New forms and textures result from the process of folding, stretching, and an astute recognition by the artist of subtle color tonalities and variants that must be controlled by lighting to achieve the desired results. Aware that the tonal palette may seem to emanate from beneath the skin's surface, Kelliher-Combs pays judicious attention to this unique artistic approach in her selection of color.

Kelliher-Combs layers her paintings by filling negative space with color using hues and tints that act to obscure a direct view inside the picture plane. Clarity of the acrylic polymer is uneven and the tonality produced by the process of folding and stretching the "skin" surface effects a diffuse pigmentation. Dark, mysterious, obscured in some areas of the work, the secret content remains teasingly veiled. With her method of handling the surface, Kelliher-Combs seems to guard personal elements buried in the layers of the viscous skin. Her acts of protecting and revealing, covering and exposing, are resistant to illumination; the themes of poignant loss, sacred trauma, and the suggestion of the profane reside within layers just below the surface.

While the visceral nature of her art might put off some audiences who are unprepared to gaze at stretched walrus stomach or seal gut (albeit embellished with delicate glass seed beads and suspended in a polymer medium), their squeamishness at the use of animal products fails to recognize the heritage of similar practices in Western culture. There is little revulsion when one considers parchment and vellum

Sonya Kelliher-Combs, *Secret Portraits*, 2002. Ink drawing on paper dipped in beeswax, 25.4 x 20.3 cm.

pages in medieval, hand-bound illuminated manuscripts made from scraped calf- or sheep-skin, or the use of human hair in Victorian mourning jewelry of the nineteenth century. Kelliher-Combs revives these almost-forgotten techniques. In *Judy's Secret Portrait* (2008), she incorporates carefully twisted, looping, free-form "lines," fashioned with human hair, tacked down with minute stitching on a paper surface dipped in beeswax. An unbroken line records a connection between two infinite points in space and time with the hair line scrolling across the surface, recoiling back on itself before resuming its forward motion.

Principally recognized as a mixed-media painter, Kelliher-Combs has a talent for drawing that is apparent in *Secret Portraits* (2002). The elliptical secret pouch form recurs as a series of lively, vigorous, and animated contour line drawings on paper. Double-sided and dipped in beeswax, the treatment allows the second drawing on the back to emerge as a shadow or ghostly "echo."[9] The wax application transforms the paper into a translucent state, melding the literal paper barrier that separates the two drawings and effectively uniting front and back in a singular image. The strong, animated graphic lines provide evidence of the artist's hand and display an intoxicating, energetic action that is visible in gestures that circle and loop across the paper, with jutting extensions twisting in multiple directions simultaneously around and through the pouch form. Displaying a playful and erotic character, the series seems the most atypical of Kelliher-Combs's artistic style, recalling instead some of the most exuberant examples of the contour drawing technique in the history of Western art, a series of nineteenth-century contour ink studies of tigers by the French Romantic painter Eugene Delacroix (1798–1863).

Kelliher-Combs is one of many new voices whose art is relevant for the next generation of Native people whose link to tribal identity is no longer defined solely by blood quantum and reservation status. She creates with fragments of stretched hides, animal skins, and textiles in serial compositions laden with subtle references that rely on older traditions yet mostly reflect the concerns of today. Embedded string, sewn materials, linear tacking, and found objects that float in layers of polyurethane acrylic medium are thought of as flotsam and debris of urban pollution. For Kelliher-Combs, however, they are select resources that best express the statements of her conscience.

Kelliher-Combs uses materials that invoke family memories and skills passed through generations of tribal practitioners along with an equal amount of other techniques and substances of Western origin. Her vision is a loving statement about place, family, and memory communicated in dynamic constructions fostering recollections of family loss, community displacement, and personal sorrow.

Sonya Kelliher-Combs, *Small White Secrets*, 2009. Acrylic polymer, cellulose, found cotton cloth, glass beads, nylon thread, variable dimensions. Collection of the artist.

Kelliher-Combs incorporates subtle cultural markers to entice viewers and invite them to examine what lies below the surface of her art, although she controls and does not permit unguarded access. She acknowledges that skin/hide is the key to revealing prejudices, stereotypes, and negative perspectives about Native people. She explains, "More recent works speak to deconstructed identity through metaphor, material, symbol, and pattern. Through the combination of indigenous materials and synthetic media, I make works that create a dialogue about this relationship."

Skin becomes a means to open windows that see out as well as in. For Kelliher-Combs, "it is a commentary on what we want people to see, but not in a literal way." The nuances and disguises that mask public and private acts remain shielded from public view; nevertheless, if left unexposed they become rife, festering and poisoning what surrounds them. Kelliher-Combs understands her responsibility to draw attention to the problems that her art reveals to the public, both inside and outside of her family and community. Sensitive to aspects of the cultures that have informed her perspective on life and art, Kelliher-Combs adds, "Problems, although challenging, must be voiced in order to transform and promote healing. Through self-expression, empowerment, community, and voices coming together we can heal from the past and move forward."[10] A legitimate voice who speaks for those who cannot, Kelliher-Combs asks for recognition and understanding through her art; her most eloquent statements are her *Secrets*, works that give insight into an individual who is reluctant to throw open the window to her soul.

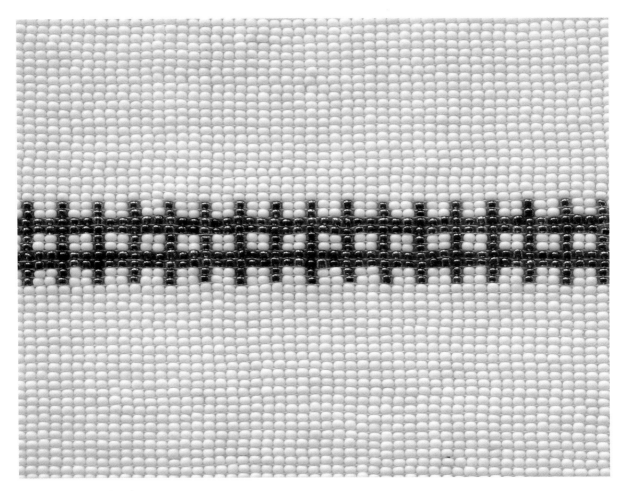

Nadia Myre, *Scarscapes* (detail),
2009. Glass beads, cotton thread,
35.6 x 10.2 cm each. Collection
of the artist. Art © Nadia Myre/
Licensed by CARCC, Ontario and
VAGA, New York.

Nadia Myre: Scarscapes

There is no subject expressing originary anguish here but a fragmented subject, pulling from past and present, innovatively producing a heterogeneous product.

—Cornel West (1988)[1]

Hannah Wilke, *S.O.S. Starification Object Series*, 1974. Photograph, 17.8 x 12.7 cm. Photo courtesy of Ronald Feldman Fine Arts, New York, © Marsie, Emanuelle, Damon and Andrew Scharlatt/Licensed by VAGA, New York, NY.

In 1974, Hannah Wilke (1940–1993) produced a provocative series of small black-and-white photographs entitled *S.O.S.—Starification Object Series*, which featured the artist posing in various states of undress, usually topless, tightly framed against a stark white background. Presenting herself in postures fluctuating between demure and playful—in one image, she wears only jeans and a cowboy hat and coyly points two toy guns toward the viewer; in another, her head is wrapped in a Muslim hijab so that only her eyes and nose are visible—the series unmistakably borrows from the language of commercial fashion photography and the oft-cited role of the female as an object for the (largely) male gaze. While the infantilization of the woman or the overt silencing of her voice evidenced by these performative images would seem to be sufficiently critical, these masquerades were only the first layer of complexity in the series and only the starting point for Wilke's aggressive undermining of what the culture deems appropriate representations of women. The artist took chewed pieces of gum and sculpted them into folded vulva-like forms (reminiscent of slightly earlier ceramic sculptures) and applied them to her upper body and face in a gesture that might best be described as grotesquerie. In hues similar to her skin tone, the strange protuberances resemble scars or growths virally attacking her otherwise flawless body.

While these seemingly unwanted and undesirable additions to Wilke's skin undoubtedly mar the superficial surface of beauty and highlight the parameters within which women are provided any amount of visibility in our culture, the artist's transgression does more than simply increase our awareness of the gender stereotypes that have long held sway over the representation of women in popular culture and the fine arts. Once the initial shock of seeing the body covered in these eruptions subsides, there is something strangely alluring about them. Each "star," as the title indicates they are named, has been carefully sculpted by Wilke, the masticated material made smooth and folded into small fleshy forms. The gum stars—carefully arranged along the spine or collarbone, mirroring one another on the cheekbones or breasts, or placed on the forehead like a *bindi*—become decorative, and the self-assuredness of the figure as she poses her adorned body suggests the possibility that a kind of ritualistic power resides in these odd little jewels.

And yet a palpable tension remains. The linguistic similarity between what Wilke chooses to call her actions—"starification"—and the word "scarification" is no coincidence. The title's acronym—"S.O.S."—carries another meaning, of course, indicative of the woman's need for help. Her confident and at times mischievous poses may be just that: they belie the distress underneath (even while it has begun bubbling to the surface). If we understand these anomalies to be scars, then the surface of the body becomes a road map of sorts, a site upon which the subject's history and the primary events of her life are manifested physically and take on pronounced visibility. Scars carry heavy emotional weight—they indicate trauma as well as survival—and the experience of seeing dozens of scars protruding from a woman's body can feel something like witnessing an unspeakable atrocity. When multiplied, the badge of honor that a single scar can symbolize transforms into a kind of disfigurement, something so intensely visceral that one is tempted to look away out of horror, pity, respect, or denial. Scars are the end point of a laceration, a physical cauterization of a wound, and their ability to make the bleeding stop can mask (to some degree) the cause of the initial trauma. In our culture, we speak of being emotionally scarred when the difficulty of an experience can never be completely forgotten and put aside. Indeed, whether physical or metaphorical, scars are reminders—evidence that we are human and can be hurt. The longer you live, the more scars you will inevitably acquire, and yet with each additional mark you may grow stronger, more resilient, and perhaps even wiser.

Montreal-based artist Nadia Myre captures beautifully the layered meanings of scars in her ongoing series *The Scar Project* (2005–present). Since 2005, Myre has held a number of workshops in which people have rendered their own scars (whether real or symbolic) by cutting and suturing raw canvas stretched onto ten-inch square frames, creating abstractions that carefully depict those imperfections of the body that we normally try to keep covered. In addition to fabricating a scar canvas, participants are asked to recall the incident that produced the wound and write down the story behind their scar. Now numbering more than five hundred pieces and still going, *The Scar Project* offers a platform whereby personal histories are transcribed within a collective action that transcends mere recollection and documentation and becomes a site for potential healing. The ongoing structure of the project, with its adherence to repetition, suggests a type of ritual that calls attention to the specificities of each person's experience while it simultaneously underscores that which is shared or common to most people. Everyone, it seems, has a scar and a story that goes along with it, whether it is the childhood fall from a bicycle or playground apparatus or something more troubling related to a surgery, accident, or altercation.

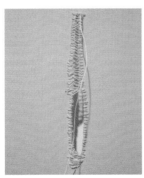

Nadia Myre, *The Scar Project* (details and installation), 2005–present. More than 500 canvases and stories written on paper, 25.4 x 25.4 x 5.1 cm each. Collection of the artist. Art © Nadia Myre/Licensed by CARCC, Ontario and VAGA, New York.

Nadia Myre, *The Scar Project* (workshop photo), 2006. Third Space Gallery, Saint John, New Brunswick, Canada.

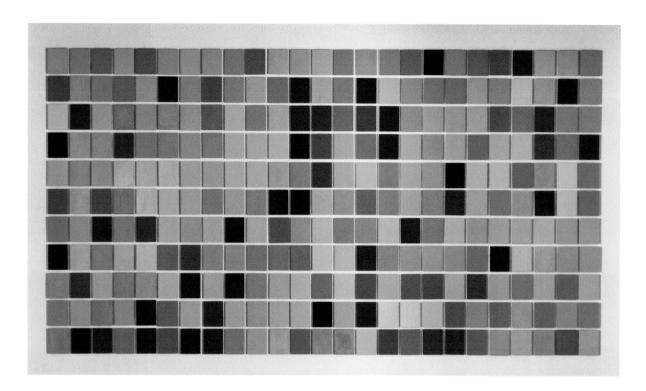

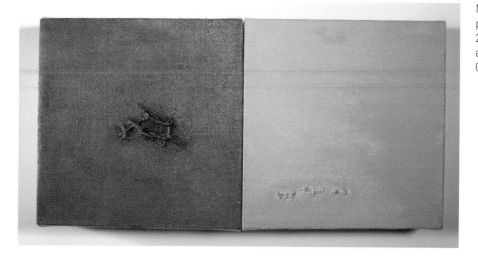

Nadia Myre, *Scar Paintings*, 2006–present. Acrylic and oil on canvas, 20 x 20 cm each. Collection of the artist. Art © Nadia Myre/Licensed by CARCC, Ontario and VAGA, New York.

OPPOSITE: Byron Kim, *Synecdoche*, 1991–92. Oil and wax on panel, 100 panels, 25.4 x 20.3 cm each.

Janine Antoni, *Loving Care*, 1993. Performance with Loving Care hair dye Natural Black, dimensions variable. Photo by Prudence Cumming Associates at Anthony d'Offay Gallery, London, 1993.

For a related project started in 2006, Myre has made a number of scar paintings that are notable, in part, for the array of exaggerated skin tones that serve as the surface to the wounds. Rather than raw canvases, these works take as their surface a monochrome painting—in deep reds, orangey yellows, bright sunburnt pinks—the pristine planes of color disrupted by the lumpy, uneven stitching. Myre's scar paintings bring to mind Byron Kim's (b. 1961) perhaps best-known work, *Synecdoche* (1991–present), a group of small abstract portraits of friends and colleagues based solely on their skin color. Kim began this series in the early nineties. Like Myre's *The Scar Project* and *The Scar Paintings* (2006–present), Kim's project is ongoing. It now consists of several hundred small monochrome panels, and he continues to add to this expanding archive of portraits. As his title describes, every panel stands in for the larger whole—an individual within an interrelated group for which Kim serves as the connecting tissue—but the uniqueness of each skin tone is never overshadowed by the whole. What is made particularly evident in this work is how our language for skin color—white, black, yellow, red—is so alarmingly inadequate. Indeed, not one of these commonplace color designations adequately describes a single person's skin tone; and the perceptible nuances and shades of pinks and browns found in the *Synecdoche* show us that each panel (and by extension, each person's skin color) is, in fact, unique.

Kim's insertion of questions of identity into the realm of abstract painting is a deliberate challenge to the formalist argument for stripping away content and reference from the medium to arrive at its so-called essence, one concerned strictly with the flatness of the picture plane and the materiality of the paint on the canvas. While personal biography was perhaps never successfully removed from the interpretation and understanding of much post–WWII painting (especially abstract expressionism), influential critic Clement Greenberg's call for the evolution of painting to reach an end point where it was concerned solely with its formal characteristics left a legacy that loomed large in American painting. Kim and peers, such as Janine Antoni (b. 1964), who riffed on Yves Klein's use of female bodies as "paintbrushes" by dipping her hair in store-bought Clairol dye and painting the floor of the gallery in her 1992 performance *Loving Care*, are intent on reconnecting the formal aspects of art to the social and political context within which it is made. Inspired by the earlier emphasis on institutional critique by artists such as Michael Asher and Hans Haacke and the urgency of issues related to feminism, civil rights, and the AIDS crisis addressed by Martha Rosler, Adrian Piper, David Wojnarowicz, and others, artists during this postmodern period in the 1990s questioned the very validity of a formalist abstraction, calling attention to the idea that meaning and interpretation cannot be divested from a work of art and its context to lie solely within a realm of self-referentiality.

Myre takes this examination of the interplay between form and content one step further to propose questions about authorship. Like Kim's *Synecdoche*, Myre's *Scar Paintings* are similarly invested in proposing skin color as a valid and primary subject within the genre of portraiture. The public aspect of *The Scar Project*, however, interestingly extends the role of the artist beyond that of strictly a maker into the realm of an instigator (we might also describe her role as that of curator or director) who creates situations in which others can actively participate as artists, too. Identity here is both shared and individualized. *The Scar Project* resists the notion of the heroic artist—the singular author—to embrace French theorist Roland Barthes's notion of the "death of the author." The artwork is not the outcome of the artist's signature gesture (Jackson Pollock's drip, for example, or Morris Louis's pour) but is an accumulation, or an amalgamation, of effort that erases "the author" as he (or she) has become widely understood in Western culture. The radicalism of this reframing of authorship is perhaps best summed up by Barthes's famous phrase, "The death of the author is the birth of the reader," wherein the reader, or the viewer, is understood to have the capacity for interpretation and the authority to prescribe meaning.[2] In this sense, *The Scar Project* belongs as much to its viewers as to its participants. Myre's commitment to creating works collectively—and specifically to organizing workshops and beading bees where people come together to make art or learn a skill—is, of course, tied to her Algonquian ancestry. Her use of activities and materials that are significant to Algonquian heritage, such as beadwork, allows her to explore her own history and identity.[3] Moreover, her commitment to collective action pays homage to the cultural and ritualistic aspects of many aboriginal peoples.

During colonial struggles and assimilation, American Indians have had to fight to keep their indigenous languages alive. Language has been a central component of Myre's practice, and she has incorporated text into her work to explore the power of language. Deconstructing how language is used to express desire and how it can be manipulated to exert authority is central to several pieces. In *The Scar Project*, the impact of visual representation is made abundantly clear by the capacity of the simulated scar to engender a range of physical reactions—empathy, remorse, shame, even pain—while the accompanying stories exemplify the way in which written language can offer elucidation yet often fails to capture the singularity of experience. In other words, as a means of expression, the descriptive quality of language has long been understood to carry certain limitations. Memory fades with time, and

Nadia Myre, *Landscape of Sorrow*, 2009. Six canvases, cotton thread, 15.2 x 213.4 cm each. Collection of the artist. Art © Nadia Myre/ Licensed by CARCC, Ontario and VAGA, New York.

the written component of *The Scar Project* is a case study of sorts in how memory functions in relationship to trauma. Each subject's emotional relationship to the event is reflected in their descriptions, which range from being coolly matter of fact to heartbreakingly candid and personal.

Myre's scar works might also be meaningfully aligned with Lucio Fontana's groundbreaking series *Concetti Spaziali (Spatial Concepts)*, which he began in 1958. In these works, commonly referred to as his "slash" paintings, Fontana took a razor to monochromatic canvases as a way to literally break through the picture plane in order to get to real space, to reality. Thus, painting's most historically valued attributes—pictorialism and representation—were disregarded and replaced with an action. And the action was nothing if not aggressive. However formally contained

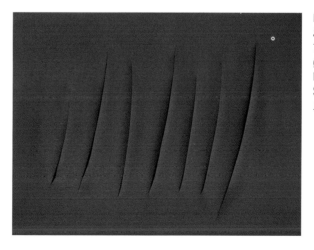

Lucio Fontana (1899–1968), *Spatial Concept: Expectations*, 1962. Oil on canvas with black gauze, 97.1 x 130.1 cm. Hirshhorn Museum and Sculpture Garden, Smithsonian Institution. Gift of Joseph H. Hirshhorn, 1966.

and beautiful these works may be, Fontana's desire to free painting of its engrained history (to, indeed, "kill" painting as it had been known) is flamboyantly on display. The canvases are at once chaotic in their forcefulness and resolved in the deliberateness of their mission. As Fontana desired, movement and time are captured by the paintings' ability to make the viewer imagine the process of their making.

Representation is more at play in Myre's *Scar Project* than in Fontana's purely abstract spatial explorations, and yet hers are not merely "representations" of scars. The works, rather, *enact* a wound and then make an actual scar through the process of mending with needle and thread. Like Fontana, Myre (and her hundreds of collaborators) cut or rip the canvas, creating pieces that are remarkably corporeal. But unlike Fontana, Myre sutures her slashes. The act of suturing, integral to this body of work, initiates a process of healing. It can also be seen as building a kind of bridge—a physical bridge between the two sides of the skin separated by a violent event, and symbolically, as in the bridging of two different cultures, generations, or ideologies. *Landscape of Sorrow* (2009), Myre's most recent scar work, consists of six thin horizontal raw canvases, hung in two stacked rows, showing long mended cuts running the length of each canvas. The scars on these canvases refer to the many scars rendered since Myre embarked on *The Scar Project* in 2005, but their elongation and movement across multiple canvases plays with scale and perspective, shifting the scars from the site of the body to the surface of the earth. These scars on the landscape represent the environmental damage inflicted by humans and underscore the fact that it is not only the human body that is vulnerable. The landscape can be irrevocably scarred by the numerous transgressions we enact upon its fragile ecosystems. The scars in *Landscape of Sorrow* seem to go on forever; they have a morose and unsettling quality when thought of as indelible markers of individual or environmental tragedies. But just as Wilke's eruptions on the skin were simultaneously grotesque and somehow beautiful, Myre's scars offer a sense of hopefulness when seen as bridges. Her optimism makes a lot of sense when one considers her life experience: Like many American Indians, she is part of two cultures—and exists between cultures—and has worked to build bridges that will connect the various parts of her identity while remaining attuned to the cultural differences. *Landscape of Sorrow* acts as a reminder of the devastation of which we are capable, but scars are also indicators of healing. Myre's work suggests that together we can effect positive change.

For the past several years, Myre has been exploring specific aspects of her Algonquian heritage as well as the larger issues of reclamation, stereotyping, and the hybridity of identity that impact all indigenous peoples living in colonized lands. In an ambitious work made over a two-year period with the help of approximately 230 volunteers, Myre adopted the traditional practice of beading to cover various sections of the fifty-six pages of Canada's Indian Act in red and white beads (the white beads were used to mask the words while the red filled in the negative spaces). Myre's *Indian Act* (2000–02) appropriately renders the contract illegible, a commentary on the prevalence of unreadable agreements between the colonial U.S. and Canadian

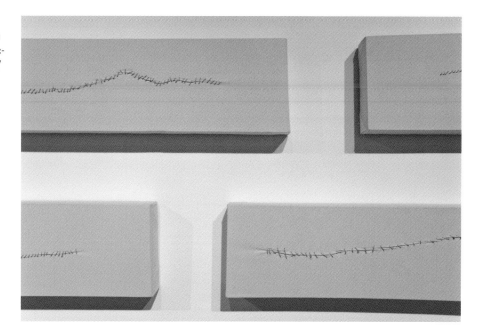

Nadia Myre, *Landscape of Sorrow* (detail), 2009. Six canvases, cotton thread, 15.2 x 213.4 cm each. Collection of the artist. Art © Nadia Myre/ Licensed by CARCC, Ontario and VAGA, New York.

governments and American Indians. Documents like the Indian Act were usually incomprehensible to those they were meant to govern and their terms often ignored or unenforced. As Richard William Hill has noted, the Indian Act was an acute "failure to communicate that was no doubt meant to communicate a great deal."[4] While the actual terms of the Indian Act in Myre's hands are now, in fact, even more unintelligible (hidden behind a decorative abstract layer of glass), the communal act of beading nonetheless functions as a kind of reclamation, allowing those who have been directly affected by the contract (or those who care about those who have been) to take ownership of it on their own terms. The artist has expressed, "I really do see beading as an act of silent resistance," and the effacement of *Indian Act* is an undeniably bold statement. As made evident in Myre's work, language per se does not hold meaning. Language must be put into action; it must move from the page out into the world. *Indian Act* animates language by calling attention to a document that has become dormant—untranslatable and ineffectual—and transfers the text from the language of the dominant hegemonic culture to that of the colonized and subjugated.

Not only does the shared physical labor of works such as *The Scar Project* and *Indian Act* importantly mirror the communal nature of Myre's Native culture's traditional art practices, but her reliance upon repetition and endurance also links her artistic process to ritual, wherein meaning is established not through language but through the physical actions of the body. The artist's investigations into language and endurance are reminiscent of the ways in which installation artist Ann Hamilton (b. 1956) has mined the terrain of language and its limitations. Writing about Hamilton's *tropos* (1993–94)—the centerpiece of which is a table and stool where a person sits and meticulously burns each word in an old book so that the text is indecipherable—curator Lynne Cooke wrote, "Experience, for Hamilton, leads to

Nadia Myre, *Indian Act* (detail, 24/56), 2000–03. Glass beads, stroud cloth, paper, masking tape, 46 x 38 x 5 cm. Collection of the artist. Art © Nadia Myre/Licensed by CARCC, Ontario and VAGA, New York.

Ann Hamilton, *tropos* (detail), 1993. Mixed media installation and performance, 464.5 sq. m. Dia Center for the Arts.

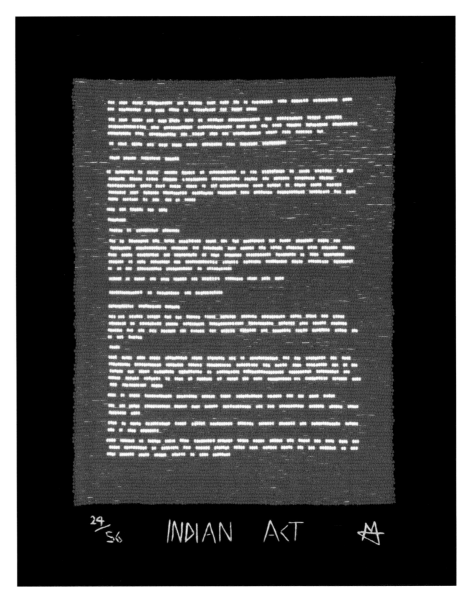

knowledge, or, more precisely, to a form of knowledge which is of far greater value and significance than mere codified information. Such knowledge comes as much through the body and the senses as through the mind."[5] Like Myre's large-scale pieces, Hamilton's multifaceted installations often require a collective effort to be realized, engendering a sense of community. Moreover, this working methodology is not solely an intellectual undertaking. Rather, it is rooted in materiality and provides an opportunity for people to learn something—to create something—through touch. Participants in Myre's *Scar Project* may be calling upon personal memories and histories but they are also creating *shared* memories rooted in a belief that the impact of their combined efforts will far outweigh each individual contribution.

In a recent video, *Inkanatatation* (2004), Myre expands her exploration of the types of marks found on the surface of the skin to provide an intimate view of tattooing. The video documents the artist getting a tattoo on her arm. Sped up to create a nearly delirious montage, the video reveals the tattoo to be three red feathers flanked by two red rectangles. Myre borrows this symbology from Mohawk artist and curator Greg Hill, who replaced the maple leaf of the Canadian flag with three red feathers in an installation and performance work in 2000. During the course of the short video, the tattoo artist continually wipes away the excess red ink and blood that comes to the surface as the skin is penetrated with the needle. The artist's tattooing of this flag, intended to honor aboriginal peoples, is a political act. Myre's title, however, also suggests that the tattoo might be part of a ritualistic spell or magic act. While incantations usually revolve around the spoken word, the repeated syllables of Myre's neologism render it nearly unspeakable (or certainly a real tongue twister). The tattoo's position as a permanent ornamentation on the skin seems to further the artist's argument that language alone cannot adequately represent experience, especially those ritualistic activities that are specific to particular cultures. Language (the very idea of an incantation) and the visual have a complex relationship here, as it does in several of Myre's works, so that the written or verbal is replaced by the visual language of an adornment to the body in the powerfully iconic form of a flag.

Though not self-portraits in any conventional sense, all of Myre's work is informed by her subjectivity. Her ability to connect her story—her identity—to her viewers' makes her work resonate far beyond any affiliations of race, ethnicity, or gender. As Cornel West argues in the epigraph for this essay, the fragmentary subjecthood with which so many of us—those who live across cultures, as aliens away from our homelands, or as residents of continuously changing societies—identify with is not necessarily a tragic crisis of identity. We have become accustomed to, and proud of, our diverse identities, our mixes and matches. We are all in some sense "heterogeneous products" of our time—collecting scars and attempting to build bridges. Nadia Myre's work can act as a compass as we each try to make our way.

Sonya Kelliher-Combs, *Watermelon
Walrus Family Portrait*, 2008. Acrylic
polymer, nylon thread, and walrus
stomach, 91.4 x 91.4 cm. Collection
of the artist.

Scene: Scars
Setting: Orca's Cabin

JAWS
(1975)

Film still from *Jaws*, dialogue courtesy of Universal Studios and Wendy Benchley.

Quint: Chief. Don't you worry about it, Chief. It won't be permanent. You wanna see somethin' permanent? Boom, boom, boom? [*Mimics punching self*] Hey, Hoop? You wanna feel somethin' permanent? Just put your hand underneath my cap. You just feel that little lump? Knocko Nolans, St. Patty's Day, Boston.

Hooper: I got that beat. I got that beat. [*Pulls up left shirt sleeve*] It's a moray eel. Bit right through my wetsuit.

Quint: Well, Hoop, now, listen. I don't know about that, but I entered an arm-wrestling contest in an Okie bar in San Francisco. You see this? [*Pulls up right shirt sleeve*] I can't extend that, you know why? Got to the semi-final, celebratin' my third wife's demise. Big Chinese fella pulled me right over! Ha!

Hooper: [*Puts leg up on table and pulls up pant cuff*] Look at that. It was a bull shark. He sc—he scraped me when I was takin' samples.

Quint: I got somethin' for ya. [*Raises right leg and pulls up pant cuff*] There's a thresher. See that, Chief? Thresher's tail. Scewp!

Brody: Thresher?

Hooper: It's a shark!

Quint: You want a drink? Drink to your leg?

Hooper: I'll drink to your leg.

Quint: Okay, so we drink to our legs! Ha ha ha!
[*Brody checks his appendectomy scar. Decides not to say anything*]

Hooper: I got the crème de la crème. Right here. Hold on. [*Unbuttons sweater collar*] Yeah, you see that?

Brody: You're wearing a sweater.

Hooper: Right there. [*Points to chest*] Mary Ellen Moffit. She broke my heart. [*Collective laughter*]

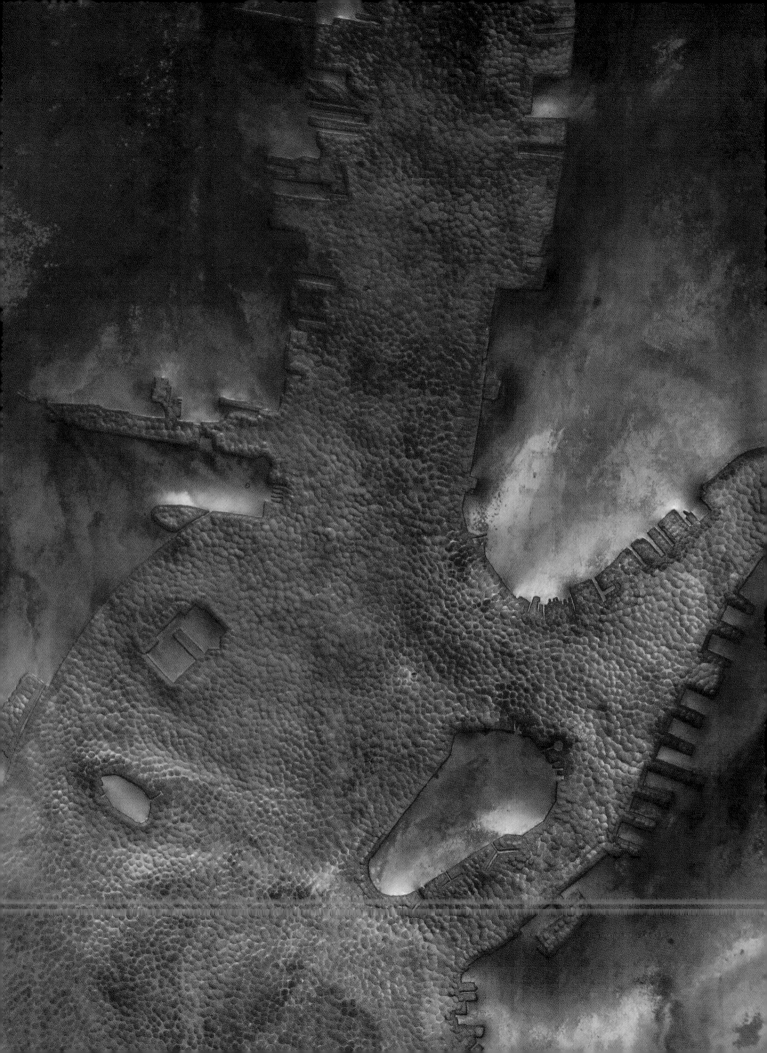

IHOR HOLUBIZKY

Michael Belmore: Shorelines, Flux, Origins, and Dark Water—the slowness of things

In his introduction to the 1980 Boyer Lectures, Australian art and cultural historian Bernard Smith quoted Clive Turnbull on the death of Truganini, the last of the Nuenone people, on Bruny Island in 1876:

> Truganini . . . had seen it all, her own story, the very story of her race. Her last years were comfortable, it seems, but there was a shadow over them—her fear of the body-snatchers and mutilation after death, . . . "Don't let them cut me up," she begged the doctor as she lay dying. "Bury me behind the mountains."[1]

Smith did not wish to dwell on the atrocities, but rather invoked this moment as a starting point for what he called "the specter of Truganini" and in turn laid the ethical groundwork through which the relationship between Aborigine culture and place—as opposed to the European settlement and conquest of *terra nullius* (the "empty land," as it was officially pronounced)—could now be examined. Truganini's wish to be buried behind the mountains—regardless of whether the story is historically accurate, or whether she was, in fact, the last Tasmanian Aborigine—speaks to me of place and belonging (i.e., the association between the land and culture/ creation mythology) as much as it might describe the desire for a "safe refuge" in the afterlife.

This preface is not meant to suggest that Michael Belmore's work addresses the vicissitudes of colonialism and history but, rather, in addition to a cultural place that predates colonialism, there is a powerful communion with place in his work and thoughts—more than is expressed by the increasingly shopworn phrase "sense of place." Belmore is cognizant of his identity not only as a person of Ojibwe heritage but also as an artist in the modern age, although not in an expected or typical way. The modern age is characterized by an obsession with speed and metaphor; speed itself can be, and has been, used as metaphor. And often, metaphors (in art and life) appear with scattergun ferocity.[2] In contrast, Belmore works in a slow tempo, or time—a consequence of his choice of materials and methods of working, includ-

Michael Belmore, *Dark Water* (detail), 2009–10. Hammered copper, steel, 304.8 x 487.7 cm. Collection of the artist.

ing taking cues from outside the urban environment—yet the outcomes are no less modern. The complexity of his work cannot be fully embodied in the four exhibition works (two were in progress at the time of this writing), but there is ample evidence from these and prior work to shape an interpretative position.

Historians, as some have said, are in the business of shaping time. The same could be said of artists; in many ways, Belmore's work does, and enacts, just that. This is not, however, just any shaping, and the exhibition title and metaphor of *HIDE* is both apt and a fact. Yet at the same time, the word raises the specter of skin in the context of a First Nations artist. The term "red Indian" is generally ascribed as originating with the Beothuk of Newfoundland, who painted their skin with red ocher; Europeans took note and wiped them out. Then, there is the reverse impact. In Inuit oral history, the appearance of the "lost" Franklin expedition of 1845 still resonates and circulates in stories kept alive by elders. The Inuit describe "how terrifying the white explorers were, their long pale faces [making] them 'otherworldly.'"[3] First contact is the "original" shock of the new, often with tragic consequences for both sides. Because of the history of power and domination, aggressive tendencies (is this human nature?) have led to discrimination, racism, and genocide based on color and "otherness."[4]

Skin—our "hide" in some vernacular usage—is the largest organ of the human body. Its biological function is to protect the internal organs but, as curator Kathleen Ash-Milby has noted in her essay in this book, animal skin was used by Native people for many things—protection from the elements in clothing and shelter, a way of surviving and being in the world. Belmore's work is not literally "in skin," to follow or "grasp tight the old ways."[5] He is fully aware of a social-cultural dimension, past and present, and employs the metaphor on his own terms. In conversation, I asked Belmore about his sense of communion with other artists, a milieu. He responded that his visual language is his own, "not in the overall art scene or even the First Nations art scene."[6] This, however, does not make him either indifferent or an iconoclast. Rather than looking over the shoulder of other artists—borrowing or adapting—Belmore's work is the solution to his own problems and challenges.

The next question I posed to Belmore concerns identity. I put forward the assertion made by philosopher Etienne Balibar in his essay "The Nation Form: History and Ideology": "All identity is individual, but there is no individual identity that is not constructed within a field of social values, norms of behaviors and collective symbols."[7] In a broad sense, a work of art can be co-opted into the "bag" of collective symbols if it serves the cult of nationalism.[8] My question was also directed to a First Nations identity and sense of belonging. Belmore responded:

> Our identity is complex [and] for the most part there is a tendency to have an Us versus Them attitude. We [all] tend to view people as "other" rather than "another." While I would agree that "all identity is individual, etc." and that this can apply to what artists do—I have a hard time seeing collective identity. It is a front; it can always be broken down, divided and turned in on itself, though usually not publicly.

Michael Belmore, *Shorelines*, 2006.
Hammered copper, 213.4 x 182.9 cm.
Collection of the artist.

To the general question of how he sees his role as an artist, Belmore replied, "I observe, I point out things—sometimes quite obvious things—for people like me to see." And rather than reject anything, Belmore noted that he "tend[s] to try and see from all points."

Shorelines (2006) puts all points to a test. Belmore has forged a map of North America over two abutted sheets of copper. The process involved heating the copper with a high-output propane torch, annealing the surface to make it malleable, and then cooling the metal before laboriously hammering it. Curator Olexander Wlasenko describes the artist's working method:

> [It] is alchemic; vacillating between determination and serendipity. Human intervention into the landscape comes with and without consequence. Belmore personalizes this conundrum in his work. . . . "I like working with copper—it's like the landscape—it's something that can be informed through calculated and miscalculated blows."[9]

Michael Belmore, *Shorelines*
(details, above and opposite), 2006.
Hammered copper, 213.4 x 182.9 cm.
Collection of the artist.

Wlasenko summarizes, "Belmore extends the ancient trajectory of his materials, infusing new life and understanding to them in a contemporary context. [His] mercurial handling of a raw material forms a vital link to a past. By preserving the inherent qualities and purity of a given material, he invokes a venerable antiquity."[10]

There are easier ways to work, and to make a map. But the form, method, and "vision" is Belmore's invention and expresses more than merely the product and sweat of his labor, as if that is the value or meaning. Belmore states, "I try to convey the 'what you see' in all [its] complexities, in its simplest form. I can't think of any actual influences anymore; art school is so far [away] from now. I tend to concentrate on my work or practice, not on the theory behind it. Hammering the copper, while

not a 'thought,' is an expression. . . . Each mark on the copper represents the strike of a hammer." Sometimes a misdirected blow can "erase" a small island.

The charting of "New World" shorelines by Europeans was not only for geographic exploration but also served as a strategic document for invasion and occupation. Belmore's strategy differs, even from the mapping that has been a subject for several artists as a conceptual stroke in the late twentieth century.[11] Any map can be viewed as a form of contract or agreement that "this is here." In a mid-1970s essay titled "Borderlines in Art and Experience," Joe Bodolai writes, "Mapping . . . is metonymical [and] no map can possibly depict all qualities of phenomena. Indeed, a map is useful precisely because it does not do this [and because it] depends on the selection and depiction of particular qualities of the mapped reality and the exclusion of others not relevant to the purpose of the particular map."[12]

In this context, Belmore's map is more than a "mere" outline of the continent; it serves another purpose in carving out what can also be regarded as an "original-conditions psychogeography."[13] The terrain stretches from the Arctic islands at the top to just above the point at the bottom where the man-made cut of the Panama Canal was drawn. The result is a land mass without national boundaries, and the only topography is the one he has generated through the physical making. There are, however, prominent inland features including the great continental lakes, the bays of Hudson and James, and the gulfs of Mexico and California, that cut into the continental mass through natural processes. The islands in the hemisphere also take on a prominence: the northern Arctic islands as noted, Newfoundland and the Atlantic islands to the east, Vancouver Island to the west (image at left), and the Caribbean islands to the south. Islands, being surrounded by water, add to the shoreline.

Each panel is seven by three feet, in a human scale, or about the size of a household door—indeed, a pair of doors and a portal that we can pass through to some other room or state of being. So, too, for the material. Not simply a medium, copper is part of our biological reality, a trace nutrient that, perversely, is poisonous in

Michael Belmore, *Flux*, 2010. River stones, gold leaf, 243.8 x 274.3 cm. Multiple installations. Collection of the artist.

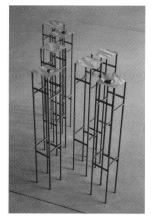

Michael Belmore, *Flow*, 2004. Sterling silver, steel, stones; Seven stands, 12.7 x 12.7 x 83.8–91.4 cm. each. Collection of the artist.

large quantities. It is used for roofing, as a conductor of electricity, and because it is malleable, in the making of household items, tools, and weapons. The metaphor is rich; in conversation he joked about his process as being akin to a "metallurgic tannery"—making a "hide." Which is to say, metaphors can be sliced thick or thin, or "hammered out" until there is no place to "hide."

Belmore's work also has a heuristic dimension. With *Shorelines*, we can project and imagine many things about biological and human history and ponder the eternal and foreverness of land and water. In doing so, Belmore sidesteps the empiricism of an authoritative map and fashions a lyricism of space, and perhaps even time, outside historical time. The inventiveness, as noted earlier, is a psychogeography of his own making and interpretation, and for us, a state of awareness. If not already obvious, this "pondering" demands patience of the viewer.

Whereas *Shorelines* presents the possibility of a grand proto-narrative, *Flux* (2010) is an organic-nature form and reflects a poetic foreverness. Ralph Waldo Emerson wrote more than 160 years ago, "We can never be quite strangers or inferiors in nature. . . . The method of nature: who could ever analyze it? That rushing stream will not stop to be observed. We can . . . never find the end of a thread; never tell where to set the first stone."[14] Belmore does, in fact, "set the first stone," and the next, and the next. *Flux* is a serpentine arrangement of water-worn river rocks on the gallery floor.[15] The rocks are a form of reclamation from a riverbed, but given a "new nature" and meaning through the intervention of carving a sympathetic contour to allow the rocks to be nested. The inside, carved surface is finished in gold leaf, but as a subtle intervention rather than a grandiose gesture. In a literal play on the exhibition title, Belmore "hides" this aspect of the work. In related works, *Landing I* and *II* (2008), only a glimpse of the carved, nestled rocks and gold leafing is visible, as a hammered copper sheet rests on top of both rock clusters. The viewer has to get down on his or her hands and knees to view and verify; this is not conventional gallery behavior.

Belmore's moment of inspiration for the work occurred at Old Woman Bay on Lake Superior, where the river flows into the bay, following a fault that was a spillway for glacial water during the last ice age, approximately ten thousand years ago. He

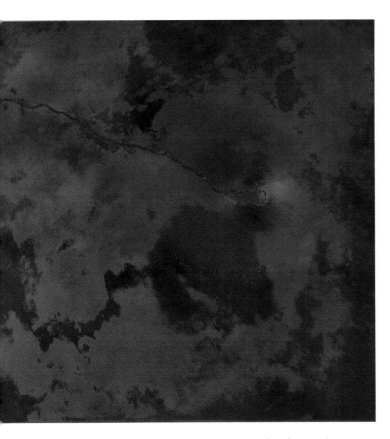

Michael Belmore, *Origins*, 2009.
Hammered copper, 30.5 x 30.5 cm.
Collection of the artist.

observed the waves receding on the shoreline, leaving brief and ever-changing foam traces. The arrangement of stones is an expression of that moment, a modeling of time and flow, which brings forward another critical aspect of Belmore's relationship to his own practice. As noted earlier, Belmore works to the slowness of things, not for the contrariness of an *arrière-garde* but in a resonance sympathetic to his observations. The flow of rivers and ocean can be observed, even compressed or arrested into a moment. The rhythms of action, however, are a cycle with no beginning or end, and therefore exceed our lifetime and ability to experience fully. Water is more than a metaphor—it is an agent, and we can know time through its effects of erosion and decay. The question, as with much of Belmore's work, is not, what can we know? but instead, how do we say and express it? Nature is reflected through the dimensions of an oral tradition in the work. By the same token, Belmore is not assuming or presuming the role of an elder. These are the choices he makes, perhaps reweaving the oft-cited quote by painter Ad Reinhardt, "Art is art. Everything else is everything else."[16] For Belmore, everything can flow into art, but not to drive a wedge between what he makes and the "everything." The challenge for the viewer is to pay attention to detail and the subtle shading. Although *Shorelines* and *Flux* may both be equitable in labor invested, conceptually linked, and even equally solid in their respective object-ness, *Flux* asks the evergreen question of the modern age: what is art? Some associative link can be made to so-called land or environmental art that first appeared in the early 1960s, but the gestures Belmore creates don't inhabit nature as monumental acts. Rather, they are meditations (on meditations) in explaining the world.[17]

Dark Water (2010) is a hybrid work, although created in a format that Belmore has used previously in *Flow* (2004). A series of hammered and dark-colored copper rectangles are mounted on functional-looking steel stands, less than a meter from the floor. The elements "map" Manhattan Island, a de facto modern city-state, yet they are separate. Hence it is "a map of the imagination." When annealed and hammered, the copper literally becomes dark (likewise for his other mapping works)—not just "tainted" water, although there is an inevitable sense of portent. Belmore observes, "The shoreline of Manhattan presents a challenge, with all those piers. Making a straight line is so much more difficult than one that meanders. The look that I am intending is that of choppy dark water."[18]

The fourth work, entitled *Origins* (2009), is a two-layered, hammered copper panel set off from the wall on pins. The small scale of the work is not a reflection of its significance or message. Geophysically, *Origins* is related to *Dark Water*. The title

Michael Belmore, *Dark Water* (detail),
2009–10. Hammered copper, steel,
304.8 x 487.7 cm. Collection of the
artist.

Michael Belmore, *Dark Water* (detail), 2009–10. Hammered copper, steel, 304.8 x 487.7 cm. Collection of the artist.

is both particular to place and leads further out, flowing into the grand narrative of nature and history. It is a map of Lake Tear of the Clouds in the Adirondack Mountains, the highest source of the Hudson River and the highest lake in New York State.[19] The lake was first recorded and mapped by the topographical engineer Verplanck Colvin in 1872, and the naming is purportedly derived from Colvin's poetic description in a journal report.[20] Mapping is a way of knowing, and research (knowing) is a critical aspect of Belmore's studio practice. His communion with place through the arterial waterways and bodies of water in North America includes his own birthplace at Upsala, west of Thunder Bay, Ontario, a region that is in the watersheds of the Arctic and Lake Superior. To the south of Upsala is Lac Des Mille Lacs (Lake of a Thousand Lakes), an important juncture for the fur trade, and, as water, significant in the history of the continent prior to European settlement. The British Royal Charter of 1670 formed the Hudson's Bay Company and assigned the commercial corporate ownership of approximately 1.5 million square miles of North America, defined in terms of proximity to the waters flowing into Hudson Bay. The vast area was virtually a country unto itself, and as a consequence the company had a dominating role in the future of Canada for the next 250 years.[21]

To state the obvious, water also plays a critical role in geological life and form, in tandem with factors of cultural consciousness and place, a topic that contemporary art writer and critic Lucy Lippard examines in her book, *The Lure of the Local*. These dynamics appear, she writes, at the "intersections of nature, culture, history, and ideology. . . . Finding a fitting place for oneself in the world is finding a place for oneself in a story."[22] The subtitle of the book, *Senses of Place in a Multicentered Society*, emphasizes the need to acknowledge the existence and persistence of local cultures rather than to view them as anachronisms in a global world. This quest for identity is echoed in Patricia Deadman's commentary on Belmore's work (and the work of Mary Anne Barkhouse): "Do we listen to the past or do we think for ourselves? How do we incorporate these shards of identity in our quest for self-determination?"[23]

The mapping that Belmore engages in is not intended to be a systematic or conceptually driven undertaking as if it is a project; he is not teaching geography. Ideas and thoughts flow, literally and metaphorically, through a personal sense of being (identity) and cultural consciousness. When asked about the stones in *Flux* and their "recontextualization," Belmore replied, "What is the stone's rightful place? Rightful is such a strong word. I can imagine a 'rightful place' for a moment, [but] I find that situation and defining how one sees oneself in relation to the world around is all so fleeting."

Postscript: Water and Skin

I am brought back to the fate of Truganini. Contrary to her wishes, she was not buried behind the mountains. Her body was taken to Hobart, buried, and later exhumed, and her skeleton put on display in the Tasmanian Museum from 1904 to 1947. Thereafter it was stored in the museum basement. In 1976, a hundred years after her death, her body was cremated through the efforts of the Aboriginal community and her ashes spread on the D'Entrecasteaux Channel, which was near her birthplace—a rightful place. In 2002, samples of her skin and hair were finally returned from the Royal College of Surgeons of England.

Terrance Houle, *Urban Indian Series* (no. 6), 2007. Eight digital C-prints, 35.6 x 27.9 cm each. Collection of the artist. Photo by Jarusha Brown.

**Sherman Alexie (Spokane/Coeur d'Alene)
interviewed by Stephen Colbert**

Colbert Report
Tuesday, October 28, 2008

Sherman Alexie, from
The Colbert Report, courtesy
of Comedy Central.

Colbert: Now what's going on politically in the Native American—Indi—Indian community—I'm going to throw them all in there, um—

Alexie: You can add "skins," too. That's the most informal thing we call each other.

Colbert: Skins?

Alexie: Skins.

Colbert: You call each other skins?

Alexie: Yes.

Colbert: I don't think I can get away with that.

Alexie: No, you can't.

Colbert: Skins?

Alexie: But I wanted to tantalize you with it.

Colbert: Skins, really? Isn't that what they call replicants in *Blade Runner*? Skins?

Alexie: Well, that's what we got it from, so, yes.

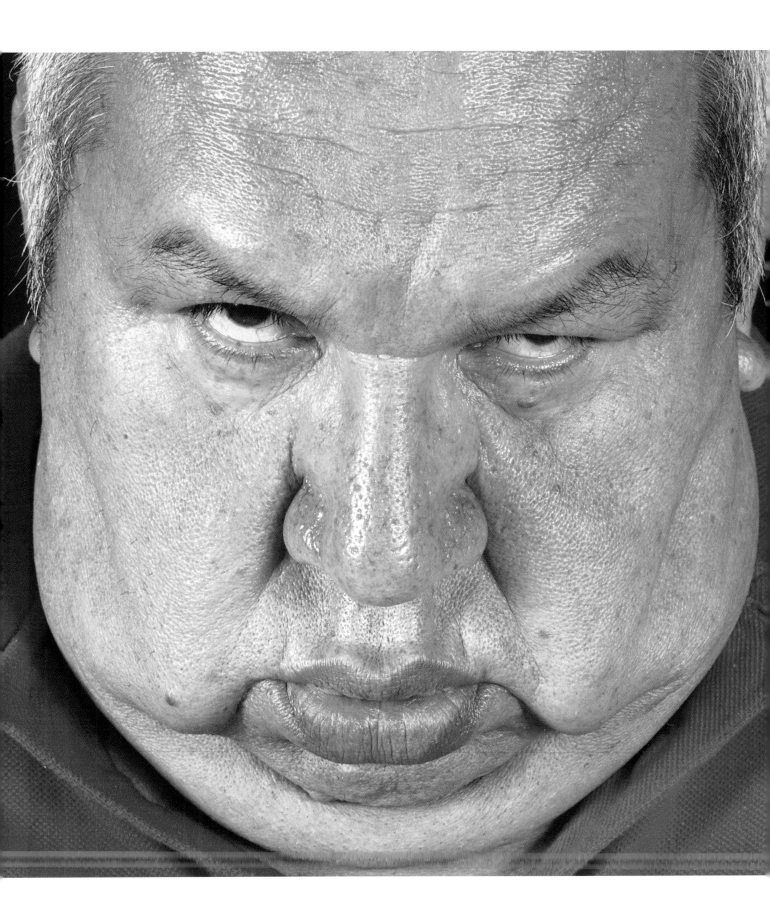

"Skin Seven Spans Thick"

HIDE is a provocative assemblage of a broad range of artistic works thematically focused on skin. The metaphoric shift from the notion of human skin to the use of the word "hide" puts this contemplation in dialogue with indigenous historic custom. The practice of using animal skins or hides by Native cultures is both an ancient and contemporary connection resulting in protective coverings. Through the work of contemporary artists in this exhibition, the focus on the exterior surface not only creates a space for interior illumination for the individual artist but also provides a glimpse for the viewer into contemporary indigenous musings.

The photographic explorations of KC Adams, Rosalie Favell, Terrance Houle, Sarah Sense, and Arthur Renwick collectively deconstruct the representation of indigenous peoples by playing with, responding to, and turning over established tropes that are recognized as part of an ongoing colonial gaze.[1] Adams, Favell, and Renwick push the genre of portraiture—a seemingly benign area of inquiry—but through their sensors and lenses they reposition indigenous bodies from the nineteenth century into the twenty-first. Houle takes on the fetishistic gaze of "Native ritual," which has eclipsed into the touristic gaze of the powwow, through a series of self-portraits. Sense appropriates pop culture and ancient traditions in a conflation of indigenous and Western technologies. Their work is in dialogue with established clichés of Native American representation in the global art world. Through this discourse, these artists reveal the philosophic underpinnings of Native indigenous cultures today.

HIDE comes after another contemporary exploration into this topic co-organized by Brian Wallis, director of exhibitions and chief curator at the International Center of Photography, New York, and the scholar/artist Coco Fusco in their explosive exhibition, *Only Skin Deep: Changing Visions of the American Self* (2005). *Only Skin Deep* constructed a diverse vision of America through the use of more than 250 photographs that revealed the tumultuous history of race representation.[2] Fusco remarks in her essay:

Arthur Renwick, *Tom*, 2006. Digital print (artist's proof, ed. of 3), 119.4 x 114.3 cm. Collection of the artist.

The photographic image plays a central role in American culture. Americans are avid producers and consumers of photographs and as our culture shifts from being predominantly print-based to image-based, we grow increasingly reliant on photographs for information about histories and realities that we do not experience directly. But we also create and use photography to see ourselves. By looking at pictures we imagine that we can know who we are and who we were. . . . No other means of representing human likeness has been used more systematically to describe and formulate American identity than photography.[3]

By examining from a perspective that neither accuses nor valorizes but rather studies their social impact, *Only Skin Deep* explores ways in which photographs make cultural classifications visible, understandable, and useful.

Fusco's insight into photography applies generally to the artists in *HIDE* with a critical exception. *HIDE* is not a seamless inclusion of these artists into an American political space, but instead locates indigenous artists within their own homelands as part of a colonial landscape in the Americas. By separating out the "Native American" artist, *HIDE* marks the conceptual territory of this exhibition as an ongoing assertion of sovereignty.[4] Native artists were included in the *Only Skin Deep* exhibition as part of the diversity of America, not as representatives of separate Native nations that predate the formation of the United States.[5] Exhibitions like *HIDE* and *Only Skin Deep* owe a debt to the space articulated by Lucy Lippard in *Mixed Blessings: New Art in a Multicultural America* (1990). This book became a standard text for undergraduate art history classes on diversity and the arts. Lippard articulated the difference between colonial settler diversity and indigenous autonomy. The recognition of Native peoples in an art book as having a specific legal relationship to the United States based on cultural difference was a significant shift from the "melting pot" analogy. *Reframings: New American Feminist Photographies* (1995), edited by Diane Neumaier, integrates photography, race, and feminist theory, and firmly installed indigenous women photographers into the discussion on gender.[6]

Overall, the category of photography has been highly problematic in its visualization and representation of Native peoples. *HIDE* provides the opportunity to deconstruct a specific historical photographic conflation of Native bodies with land. The dispossession or occupation of thousands of acres of Native land is visualized in the photograph as both an absent and primitivized Native subject. *HIDE* shifts the discussion from the corporal body, which signifies physical occupation, to the conceptual space of skin, or perhaps to a philosophical rejection and penetration of the West. Therefore, this mapping of skin rejects colonial constructions and expands and renegotiates a framing that has the potential to serve indigenous desire.

Arthur Renwick's work is the most overt in its confrontational reproduction of the face. There is perhaps an unintended transparency in the work of Adams, Favell, and Renwick because their subjects are often other indigenous people in the arts. This kind of collaboration is noted specifically within Renwick's portrait of

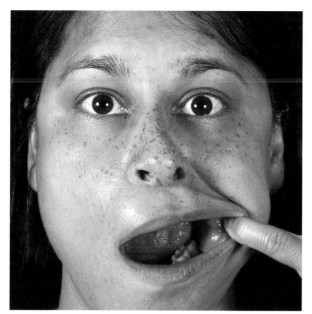

Arthur Renwick, *Michelle*, 2006.
Digital print (ed. 1/3), 119.4 x 114.3
cm; *Danny*, 2006. Digital print (ed.
1/3), 119.4 x 114.3 cm. Collection of
the artist.

Tom Hill (Seneca, p. 80), one of the most important arts professionals within the
Canadian and Haudenosaunee markets. Hill transformed artistic growth within
the Six Nations community near Brantford, Ontario, and consulted on the agendas
for Washington's National Museum of the American Indian and the Canadian
Museum of Civilization in Gatineau. Renwick's attempt to subvert noble and stoic
responses to the camera was his leading creative impulse. The intention of the artist to undermine the reduction of the individual by stereotyping may have created
a latent connection to both indigenous traditions and Western primitivism. The
resulting image of Tom Hill has a sublime quality similar to the *hodii*, the tradition
of false faces worn by members of curing societies among the Haudenosaunee, and
the Northwest Coast mask-making traditions. The tight framing of the face, direct
frontal posture, stripped-down color palette, large scale of the print, and extreme
gestural expressions reinforce masked dance traditions that obscure rather than
recover the individual. Ironically, the willingness of the subject to contort reveals
the transformational quality of these individuals. The traditional use of masks has
always been about transformation, and on this level the series is highly effective.

At almost the opposite end of the spectrum, portraits by Rosalie Favell titled
Facing the Camera (2008–present) also document Canadian Aboriginal and international indigenous artists and curators. These images are a direct counternarrative
to the profusion of nineteenth-century ethnographic portraiture that defined the
stoic, noble Indian stereotype. Favell's desire to document her community through
art recuperates indigenous agency. Her inclusion of herself in this series is a subtle
intervention on "supermodernity," or what anthropologist Marc Augé identified
as "the shift of gaze and plays of imagery . . . a modern form of solitude."[7] Augé's
characteristics of supermodernity are incoherently perceived places that we "inhabit
when driving down the motorway . . . or sitting in an airport lounge waiting for

the next flight to London," sometimes demarcated with codified ideograms like road signs, maps, and tourist guides, but always generic non-places.[8] Favell's series of portraits identifies a specific community of artists within an urban setting. Many in this community are Aboriginal but not all; her portraits are an interventionist reflection of Augé's supermodern places.

Favell's insertion of herself in this series is significant because she represents a new construction of twenty-first-century Native identity. Her articulation of the future, first and foremost, recognizes the indigenous community as fluid, not confined by reserved colonial space. She marks it as a shared urban space that contains a dynamic community in which she insinuates herself as part of reworking the photographic dilemma of subject/object authorities. Her artistry with the medium of photography demonstrates a delicate restraint of saturated light to achieve a sense of volume, thereby visually dispelling the flattened space of Indian stereotypes and reconstituting the Indian as multidimensional. Her portraits humanize each subject with warm-tones on an austere backdrop with soft, low-key lighting, which creates both an acknowledgment and recognition of the importance of individuality. Favell's self-portrait underscores her recovery of her sense of place within a Native community by creating a collective indigenous non-place for the images to reside.

KC Adams, *Cyborg Hybrid Cody*, 2009. Digital print, 50.8 x 35.6 cm. Collection of the artist.

Where Favell seeks to recognize the humanness of "being," KC Adams confronts the technological interventions in play on bodies today. She accomplishes this by merging the ever-present Indian issue of "mixed ancestry" with Donna Haraway's *Cyborg Manifesto* (1985) in her *Cyborg Hybrid Series* (2004–present).[9] The highly codified parameters of her aesthetic reinforce the idea of mixed ancestry as an ongoing experiment. The rigid formula of the all-white T-shirt, puff of fur on the collar, beaded text statements, and thinly beaded bone chokers contrasted with the highly saturated color of the skin tone and overly directed poses make Adams the "creator" of these portraits. The term "creator" is used in much the same way bioperformance

KC Adams, *Cyborg Hybrid Renzo*, 2009. Digital print, 50.8 x 35.6 cm. Collection of the artist.

artist Stelarc (b. 1946) envisions the body not as a subject but as an object for redesigning and merging with technology for postevolutionary needs.[10] Adams's work is in simultaneous dialogue with Edward S. Curtis's iconic early twentieth-century portraiture of Native people and Richard Avedon's fashion advertising shots. This convergence of technique and technology results in seductively elegant portraits of Native artists. The inherent beauty of the images makes it difficult to view them as an intervention into colonial narratives. But make no mistake, these imbricated photographs provide a visual and conceptual gloss that force a reevaluation of a contemporary indigenous contact zone.

Adrian Stimson, *Terrance*, 2009.
Ferrotype (collodion wet plate),
10.1 cm x 12.2 cm. Collection of
the artist.

Another indigenous artist on the horizon, Adrian A. Stimson (Siksika, b. 1964),
also creates a bridge between the ongoing deconstruction of Curtis's work and the
artists in *HIDE*. Stimson's *Portraits from Turtle Island Human Life* (2009), collodion
wet-plate portraits of contemporary Native and non-Native people, are both conceptually and aesthetically in conversation with Curtis. Stimson's portraits of Terrance
Houle and others share the same stylistic oeuvre as Curtis but shift the meaning
because the viewer is forced to consider these individuals as contemporaries. His
work acts as an important aesthetic and conceptual link between the authority of
Curtis's work and the recovery of indigenous autonomy.

Renwick, Favell, and Adams all maintain a stylized artistic structure with very different outcomes. Both Renwick and Adams remove then transform the individual in their vision of the future. Renwick's exaggerated features and faces demonstrate self-confidence through the act of self-deprecation. Adams culls from the modes of popular culture while taking on the extreme vulnerabilities of the place of individuals within indigenous communities; she situates her subjects in the milieu of youth culture and at the same time exposes the ugly political issue of recognition. Favell's portraits construct the new communities of Native people with confidence and humanity. Each artist in some way presents the new faces of indigeneity through the established genre of portraiture. A number of artists are collaborating with their subjects as part of the photographic process. The impulse to collaborate or seek willing consent from their participants is no doubt a counter-objectification strategy. It allows the artists a wider berth of creative interpretation while it deconstructs the historic colonizing gaze.

Blood multimedia artist Terrance Houle's *Urban Indian Series* (2007) recovers the layered meaning in the role of tradition in indigenous communities by repositioning powwow-style outfits within the mundane. During the nineteenth century, the camera witnessed the Blood, Lakota, and Blackfeet Nations of the Great Plains in transition from a Native hegemony to an accommodation of European ideas and material culture. The nineteenth-century intersection between photographic technology and aggressive American and Canadian colonization strategies penetrated deep into the Plains tribal territories and resulted in the formation of the image of the "iconic Indian." It was during this encounter that aboriginal peoples throughout the Plains transformed traditional ceremonies into what we understand today as the "powwow." This form of Native modernity captivated the imagination of the anthropological lens while sustaining Native cultures. The eagle feather headdress, cascading fringe, and beaded geometrics all signify an imaginary visual so powerful that it continues to stand in for all "Indians."

In his *Urban Indian Series* photographs, Houle strips the viewer of the unmediated pleasure of the touristic gaze within the powwow setting as he commutes on the subway, selects a new DVD, or kisses his wife good-bye, all in full regalia. Similar to Coco Fusco and Guillermo Gomez-Pena's *Year of the White Bear and Two Undiscovered Amerindians Visit the West* (1992–94), James Luna's *The Artifact Piece* (1987),

Zig Jackson (Mandan/Hidatsa/Arikara, b. 1957), *On the Bus*, from the *Indian Man in San Francisco* series, 1994. Gelatin silver print, 40.6 x 50.8 cm.

and Zig Jackson's *Indian Man on the Bus* (1994), Houle's work deconstructs primitivism. By locating his Blood traditions in everyday occurrences, the artist confronts the space for indigeneity in the twenty-first century. In contrast to the fictive "Indians" in *Two Undiscovered Amerindians*, Houle incorporates his Blood Nation heritage and powwow dancer practice into a discussion of his work. Clearly, the images are not simply about interrupting the touristic gaze. Houle's *Urban Indian Series* pushes back against the flattening process

Terrance Houle, *Urban Indian Series* (no. 3), 2007. Eight digital C-prints, 35.6 x 27.9 cm each. Collection of the artist. Photo by Jarusha Brown.

of stereotyping and exoticism in a slightly different way by shedding layers of his traditional outfit to expose his skin in the bedroom and bathroom scenes (pp. 37 and 119). The exposure of his skin is analogous to Luna's own display in the archetypal installation *The Artifact Piece* as a deconstruction of colonialism. Houle's work, however, additionally affirms indigenous traditions through peeling off the evidence of difference while remaining connected through the casually discarded, yet within reach, regalia by the bath and a gestured embrace of the vest while dressing. Houle's familiar physique and stalwart demeanor suggests both confidence and openness. One hundred and eighty degrees from the position of "no photography without our permission," both images take the viewer into personal space, in contrast to their context of public space. The artist exposes his skin to emphasize shared commonality while juxtaposing evidence of an indigenous worldview through his powwow outfit. The *Urban Indian Series* frames these two views, leading the viewer

Terrance Houle, *Urban Indian Series*
(nos. 4 & 5), 2007. Eight digital
C-prints, 35.6 x 27.9 cm each.
Collection of the artist. Photos by
Jarusha Brown.

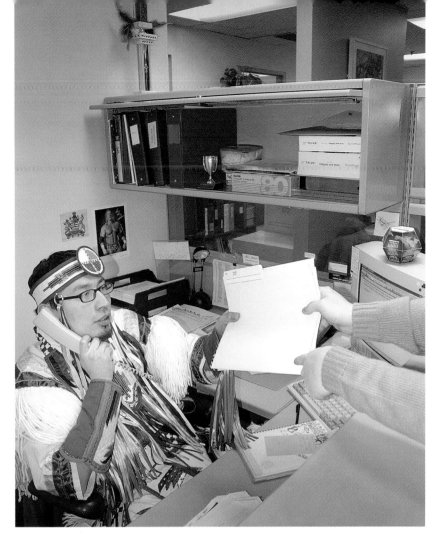

Dinh Q. Lê, *Untitled 9* (*From Vietnam to Hollywood Series*), 2004. Woven photographs printed on Fuji professional color paper, 80 x 170 cm.

OPPOSITE: Sarah Sense, *Karl 2* (above), and *Karl 3*, 2009. Digital prints on paper and mylar, artist tape, 121.9 x 243.8 cm. Collection of the artist.

from the position of the negotiation of an indigenous space in the Americas to the realization that Native worldviews are within the mind and the spirit, sheltered by our skin.

Sarah Sense uses digital prints, appropriated pop culture imagery, and self-portraits to create photographic weavings not unlike the well-known work of Vietnamese artist Dinh Q. Lê (b. 1968). Both Sense and Lê integrate the traditional knowledge of basketweaving from their respective cultures with photographic topics on Hollywood and violence. This confluence of experiences is represented through Sense's conceptual and production processes. The weavings are simultaneously evolving the object-ness of both photography and indigenous cultures. The remix that Sense, like Adams, has created positions the challenge of an indigenous presence with contemporary technologies.

In her work, Sense is influenced by her maternal legacy from the Chitimacha of Louisiana and her paternal German heritage. After a Southern Californian childhood, Sense ended up in a forward-thinking art school and was encouraged to investigate her cultural subjectivities. She grew up with baskets in her home but knew little else about her indigenous heritage; the basket became her entry point. Like many disenfranchised Native people before her, she began the process of creating a connection to the community of Chitimacha in Louisiana. Sense purchased a basket, which she identified as having two patterns—Robin's Foot and Raven-Eye—which she incorporated in her weaving of mats and baskets.

Sense's work is further enriched by her emotional tie to a physicist grandfather she never really knew. She has described this man as an archive of equations. It was a happenstance encounter at the Banff Centre in Alberta, Canada, with another mathematician that provided the theoretical justification for incorporating numerical sequences in her recent work *Karl* (2009). She imagines prime numbers and periodic tables as another base grammar for her weavings.

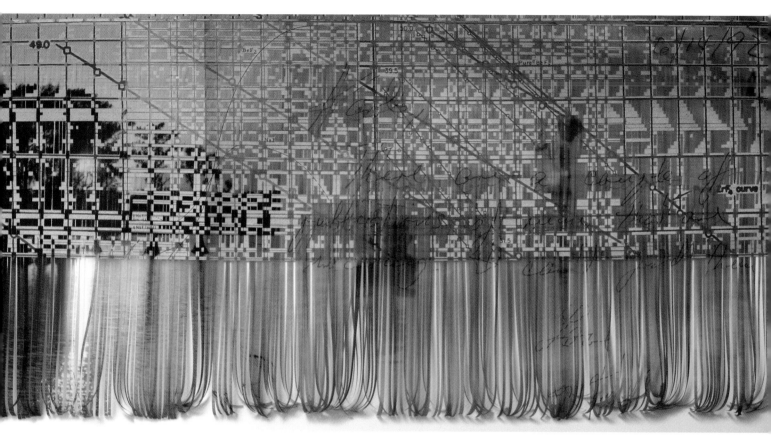

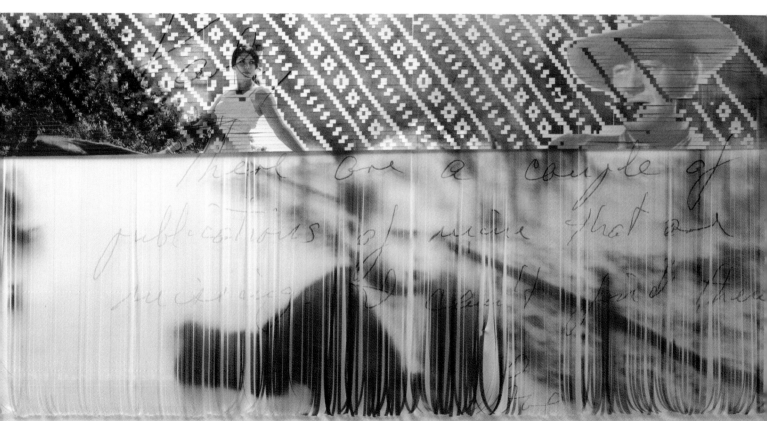

Although Sense has direct familial ties with the use of baskets and recognizes the mathematical logic of weaving and science, this connection is more about personal motivation. Her keen eye moves the observation of aesthetic and numerical patterns into a sharp critique on contemporary society by dissecting well-known photographic images. Her rhythmic patterns of images shred conventional American stereotypes of Indians and remake the whole as a kind of pastiche of contemporary indigenous culture. Sense continues to integrate landscape, the dominant genre of photography, into her work, except her version is a transcultural fusion of Chitimacha spatial ordering, Western science, and Hollywood hegemony. The objects she creates are accurate summations of the layered locations of contemporary indigenous peoples, rather than flat two-dimensional surfaces. Ella Shohat and Robert Stam articulate "people of culture" as a way of creating a distinction between discrete cultural framings and the hegemony of the West in *Unthinking Eurocentrism* (1994).[11] The term "culture" is really what the work of most indigenous artists examines. It consistently resurfaces as the tablet upon which the messages are scribed. The work of Sarah Sense weaves all of these spaces together while magnifying the spatial and conceptual differences.

Sarah Sense, *Kart 2* (detail), 2009. Digital prints on paper and mylar, artist tape, 121.9 x 243.8 cm. Collection of the artist.

The artists selected for *HIDE*'s photography section understand not only that their work is part of a global conversation but that it is anchored by colonial tropes of primitivism, Orientalism, academic marginalization, and nation-state erasure. Their work challenges the nineteenth-century regime of imagery that continues to define Indians while it inserts into the mix a new sense of being indigenous. The work of Native photographers from previous generations had agency but was not a direct act of decolonization. The artists in this exhibition, on the other hand, express an overt authority to claim jurisdiction over the ongoing construction of indigeneity.

Skin or hide acts as a kind of essential blank slate where artists inscribe their visions of experience, projected as racial and philosophical difference. The work of all of these artists is negotiated through the relationship to their own multiple heritages, in which "indigenousness" is a complicating factor. In other words, they are all in dialogue with a central construction of indigeneity as part of their negotiation of personal space, with skin or hide as a dominant visual and conceptual component. Their impulse to contemplate this surface as a means to understand the experience of being indigenous in the world today is both apt and profound.

Perhaps some do not understand this surface's power, but it is a founding concept of leadership amongst the Haudenosaunee of the northeastern woodlands. Mohawk elder Tom Porter recounts in *And Grandma Said*, "You have to have skin seven spans thick." This thought has always been part of my own history as a common phrase used to express the expectation of leaders to be both compassionate and strong. In this case, the metaphor of "skin" relates directly to an animal hide. When a deer is skinned, the hair is removed; if it is not tanned, it becomes rigid. The responsibilities of a leader are so challenging that it takes seven of these hardened hides to protect the chiefs against the pressures of their roles. "Skin seven spans thick" is both a physical and psychological barrier against harm, allowing leaders to absorb the words of frustration from their people while continuing to express compassion.[12]

Communities like the Haudenosaunee maintain cultural borders through the strength of chiefs and clan mothers, but leadership has many faces. It can be found in multiple locations as Indian Country undergoes reconstruction to accommodate communities that are postreservation, diasporic, and urban. The permeable space for indigeneity today is reflected in the concerns of the artists represented in *HIDE*. Exhibitions like *HIDE* are integral keystones of the theoretical shift from deconstruction to reconstruction. Photography represents our continued dialogue with both modernity and ocular technology. The sites of reference in this exhibition negotiate cultures that predate the formation of the United States by more than a thousand years. The integration of the onset of modernity and various technologies are not a seamless fit yet are accommodated through the innovation of the artist. *HIDE* marks a transitional moment in indigenous experiences because each artist relocates indigenous bodies into the future with strength and empathy. The photographers in *HIDE* dare to hold up the proverbial mirror for the viewer to encounter the past, recognize the present, and unveil our future.

(1) and (2),

case the Minister is satisfied that any children of
adequately provided for, he may direct that all or any
ould otherwise go to the widow shall go to the

that the widow shall have the right, during her
nds in a reserve that were occupied by her deceased
eath.

leaving issue, his estate shall be distributed,
widow, if any, per stirpes among such issue.

other

leaving no widow or issue, his estate shall go to
al shares if both are living, but if either of them
o the survivor.

sters and their issue

leaving no widow or issue or father or mother, his
among his brothers and sisters in equal shares, and
ds dead the children of the deceased brother or
their parent would have taken if living, but where
e children of deceased brothers and sisters, they

leaving no widow, issue, father, mother, brother or
deceased brother or sister, his estate shall go

he next-of-kin, it shall be distributed equally
equal degree of consanguinity to the intestate and
nt them, but in no case shall representation be
nd sisters' children, and any interest in land in a
Majesty for the benefit of the band if the nearest of
e remote than a brother or sister.

s section, degrees of kindred shall be computed by
testate to the nearest common ancestor and then
d the kindred of the half-blood shall inherit
whole-blood in the same degree.

orn after intestate's death

ves of an intestate begotten before his death but
it as if they had been born in the lifetime of the
him.

RICHARD WILLIAM HILL

After Authenticity: A Post-Mortem
on the Racialized Indian Body

The margins, our sites of survival, become our fighting grounds and their site of pilgrimage. Thus, while we turn around and reclaim them as our exclusive territory, they happily approve, for the division between margin and center should be preserved, and as clearly demarcated as possible, if the two positions are to remain intact in their power relations.

—Trinh T. Minh-ha (1990)[1]

The idea of exploring hide and skin as metaphors for the slippery questions of indigenous representation and self-presentation strikes me as timely. It evokes questions about the relationship between a postmodern interest in surface and the field of representation versus a modernist insistence on depth and essence. For indigenous peoples these terms also have racialized associations, and discourses of race inevitably collapse distinctions of surface and essence. For the racist the surface, the amount of melanin in the skin, tells one all one needs to know about the essence, which is often said to be carried deep in the blood. It is timely to revisit the questions of race and essences because we are at a moment in which curators Gerald McMaster (Plains Cree) and Joe Baker (Delaware), through the exhibition *Remix: New Modernities in a Post-Indian World* (2007), have recently declared our current situation to be one of (not always acknowledged) cultural hybridity. Of course the many artists and art scenes that make up the indigenous art world have no organ of communication through which official announcements or manifestos are disseminated, but when senior curators like McMaster and Baker, representing at the time of the exhibition's conception the Smithsonian and the Heard Museum respectively, it can be said with confidence that the issue has been placed squarely on the table.

In the catalogue for the exhibition, hybridity is proposed as an antidote for a series of dated essentialisms that freeze indigenous cultures in a romanticized past, alienating us from full engagement with the larger world. McMaster locates this particularly in the changing cultural circumstances of a new generation of artists, many of whom are of mixed heritage, that are creating a crisis for those for whom "cultural identity has been so important, and so often focused on appearances."[2]

Nadia Myre, *Indian Act* (detail, 25/56), 2000–03. Glass beads, stroud cloth, paper, masking tape, 46 x 38 x 5 cm. Collection of the artist. Art © Nadia Myre/Licensed by CARCC, Ontario and VAGA, New York.

Or, in other words, focused on assumptions that conflate race and identity. This is a conversation we need to have and, as these curators suggest, in a way that is informed by our complex histories and present circumstances.[3]

The term "hybridity," as McMaster and Baker use it, emerged from the context of British cultural studies and postcolonial theory; its most notable proponent has been theorist Homi K. Bhabha. Bhabha has attempted both to explore the way in which hybridity disturbs fixed colonial identities as well as to articulate and value experience across and between cultures (rather than within protected nationalist essentialisms) that have arisen out of the colonial period and its aftereffects of decolonization, immigration, and neocolonialism.[4] One of the difficulties with hybridity as a metaphor is that it implies a model in which two discrete cultures are stitched together to make a new, two-part entity. In the colonial situation, where cultures that have developed in long periods of isolation before coming into contact, this model makes a certain sense, but it can also distract us from the fact that each side in the colonial encounter was already a culture in transition and that cultures are always already hybrid, having no pure state of origin. Therefore, the term is useful in helping us recognize the complex linkages and exchanges that compose culture, but in a sense the condition of hybridity is simply culture working as a medium of exchange and change as culture always does. That said, there is a danger that a celebration of hybridity can devolve, in the absence of critical self-reflexivity, into the worst sort of postmodern promiscuity of signs in which aspects of culture are appropriated and deployed without concern for their history or situation within relations of power.

To engage the question of skin and blood or surface and essence, I want to revisit the construction of the essentialized and racialized discourse of the Indian in the history of North American colonization before exploring the complex ways in which ideas of race and essence were both unselfconsciously adopted by some late twentieth-century Indian activists and resisted by others. In particular I wish to read the attempts to construct an essential Indian identity not as a straightforward return to origins and tradition, as its proponents claimed, but as a complex and often unconscious mimetic return to some of the central ideas of nineteenth- and early twentieth-century European racism. I will argue that the founding of modern ideas of indigenous authenticity was contaminated from the beginning, at the deepest structural level, that of language, by colonial racism. At the same time, there were those who rejected these notions of identity. One of the earliest and most eloquent was artist and former American Indian Movement (AIM) activist Jimmie Durham. As Durham and many others have argued, indigenous North Americans live within a "framework of unreality"—a systematically misrepresentative series of discourses that have arisen out of the power dynamics of the colonization of the Americas.[5] Thanks to Hollywood Westerns we are extraordinarily recognizable, but that visibility is almost entirely a fiction.

Europeans, and later the settler colonists in the Americas, desperately needed the Indian to complete their conception of themselves as the vanguard of civilization. They needed the Indian so badly that they invented his prototype long before Columbus. George Boas and Arthur O. Lovejoy's brilliant 1935 study *Primitivism and Related Ideas in Antiquity* reveals the extent to which the concept of the dichotomy between the primitive and the civilized, which was how Europeans came to conceptualize their encounters with indigenous peoples, long precedes European engagement with indigenous America. In their meticulous analysis of texts from classical antiquity, Boas and Lovejoy identified the prototypes of the major tropes that would be deployed in European colonial attempts to understand the Indian as primitive. Thus the primitive could be a dangerous savage unrestrained in his natural hedonism, or a positive figure, a noble savage disciplined by primitive necessity according to the essential norms of nature.[6] Boas and Lovejoy even find the prototype of the nineteenth century trope of the "vanishing Indian" in antiquity: "It was despondently recognized by some ancient and many modern writers that the disease of civilization could not be prevented from spreading—that it must eventually infect even those who had thus far, through a fortunate isolation, escaped it."[7]

At the time of Columbus's contact with the Americas, Europeans also had an active folk mythology of the primitive in the form of the "wild man" and other bestial hybrids in quasi-human shape that frolicked in the margins of medieval art, from drolleries on illuminated manuscripts to small sculptures beneath misericords.[8] These images of hairy wild folk and other creatures engaging in cannibalism and wanton sexuality, including the captivity of Christian women, became prototypes for early images of the Indian. In her essay "The Wild Man and the Indian in Early 16th Century Book Illustration," Susi Colin argues that specific images of the wild man were directly adapted to create the first images of Indians distributed in Europe. We can note, for example, that, like the hairy wild man, early illustrations of the Indian show him bearded and engaged in unbridled sexuality and cannibalism.[9] In one image meant to illustrate an account of Brazilian Indians, two Indians can be seen wandering in a forest populated by unicorns, the wild woman's frequent companion.

Given this history of representation, it becomes evident that our identities have been framed since contact within hierarchical dichotomies developed prior to any experience of our particular cultures. The most significant of these dichotomies are: nature versus culture, primitive versus civilized, or heathen versus Christian. In the nineteenth century these dichotomies were given a modern gloss with emergence of pseudoscientific racism—ideas of white racial superiority, with positive (intelligent, advanced, civilized) and negative (dull, primitive, savage) aspects of character believed to be transmitted along racial lines. These "racial characteristics" were first said to be carried "in the blood" and with the development of genetic theory, in the genes. During the latter half of the nineteenth century, salvage anthropology and other self-defined documenters of the "vanishing Indian" created a distinction between the "authentic" Indian and those who had been rendered inauthentic and uninteresting through acculturation. In this context the dichotomies that had long governed our identities were easily reversed into "positive" versions of the same tropes—the savage could become the noble savage, the doomed critic of the corruption of civilization—without ever escaping from the fundamental assumptions of these categories.

Celluloid Skin

Film still from *The Silent Enemy*, 1930, directed by H.P. Carver. Buffalo Child Long Lance is the bare-chested "Indian." Chauncey Yellow Robe and an unidentified actor are also shown.

The Silent Enemy, directed by H. P. Carver, was released in 1930. The film focused on the struggles of an Ojibwa community over a harsh winter. In this publicity still, many of the stereotypical markers of Native identity are present, including the buckskin clothing and the ubiquitous bare-chested brave. Baluk, the romantic lead pictured here, was played by Sylvester Long, known at the time as Buffalo Child Long Lance (1890–1932), a minor Indian celebrity popular in New York high society, whose adventurous childhood traditionally raised among the Blackfoot was detailed in his autobiography *Long Lance* (1928). Soon after the film's release, Long gained notoriety as a famous Indian "impostor" after investigations revealed that he was not the son of a Blackfoot chief nor Cherokee as he had claimed. Raised in a mixed-race home of African-American, Native American, and European heritage in the racially polarized American South, his personal history was far more complicated than the cultural norms of the early twentieth century would recognize. However, Long did have the superficial attributes such as bronze skin color and high cheekbones that allowed him to fulfill the "Noble Indian" stereotype for his patrons, as well as the wherewithal to use these to his advantage.[*]

---

[*]   For more information about Long Lance see Donald B. Smith, *Chief Buffalo Child Long Lance: The Glorious Impostor* (Red Deer Press, 1999); and Donald B. Smith, *Long Lance: The True Story of an Impostor* (Toronto: Macmillan of Canada, 1982).

Rosalie Favell, *Ron Noganosh*, 2009.
From the *Facing the Camera* series,
digital print, 61 x 50.8 cm. Collection
of the artist.

During his time in the American Indian Movement, Durham watched the movement's growing relationship with counterculture romanticism, particularly around spirituality, with dismay.[10] He saw AIM's decline as being tied to this retreat into romanticism and away from serious politics. He wrote:

> The U.S. has used romanticism more effectively to keep Indians oppressed than it has ever been used on any other people. The basis of that romanticism is of course the concept of the "Noble Savage," but the refinements over the years have worked their way into how *every* non-Indian thinks about us, and how we think of ourselves.[11]

In "The Ground Has Been Covered," his first essay in *Artforum*, Durham struggled with the conundrum of having no place or viable identity from which to speak and enter the art discourse. "I feel fairly sure that I could address the entire world if only I had a place to stand. You [white Americans] have made everything your turf. In every field, on every issue, the ground has already been covered."[12] Mocking the romantic stereotypes of the noble savage, he assured his audience that he occupied a position of known-in-advance but paradoxically absolute alterity:

> Don't worry—I'm a good Indian. I'm from the West, love nature, and have a special, intimate connection to the environment. (And if you want me to, I'm perfectly willing to say it's a connection white people will never understand.) I can speak to my animal cousins, and believe it or not I'm appropriately spiritual.[13]

Under these circumstances, all of the usual routes forward are strewn with colonial traps. If you propose a counternarrative it will simply be absorbed into the discourse on the Indian by those in charge of managing knowledge about us. All the better if the narrative is tragic, as there is already a long tradition of whites "being entertained by the sorrows" of indigenous peoples.[14] If you retreat into ethnic nationalism you forfeit the right to be part of the world and become a defender of the past rather than an agent of the future. As Durham said, "My intention . . . is always to be a person in the world: the entire world as it is. That was the Cherokee reality before the enclosure."[15]

Alternatively, you can sell the idea of your authenticity by creating arts and crafts that conform to the dominant culture's notion of authentic Indian art. Durham attempted to disrupt this salvage paradigm-inspired desire to freeze authenticity in the past by offering a dynamic interpretation of tradition, a term that is often used in discourse about indigenous art to distinguish pre-and post-Contact cultural practices. He wrote:

> Traditions exist and are guarded by Indian communities. One of the most important of these is dynamism. Constant change—adaptability, the inclusion

of new ways and new material—is a tradition that our artists have particularly celebrated and have used to move and strengthen our societies. . . . By participating in whatever modern dialogues are pertinent we are maintaining that tradition.[16]

Yet Durham worried that we ourselves, in the confusion and trauma of an ongoing, grinding struggle, were in danger of succumbing to the persistent nineteenth-century discourse of authenticity. In the introduction to a book of his poetry, he wrote:

> One of the most terrible aspects of our situation today is that none of us feel that we are authentic. We do not think that we are real Indians. But each of us carries this "dark secret" in his heart, and we never speak about it. . . . The stereotype says to us that an Indian is a person who does and thinks certain things, within a very well-defined parameter that is like a wall around the Garden of Eden.[17]

In his book *Mimesis and Alterity*, Michael Taussig argues that mimesis is an important means by which culture is transmitted and reproduced. In encounters with radical cultural difference the processes of mimicry become "'a space between,' a space permeated by the colonial tension of mimesis and alterity, in which it is far from easy to say who is the imitator and who is the imitated, which is the copy and which is the original."[18] In these instances of "second contact," Taussig argues, "the border has dissolved and expanded to cover the lands it once separated such that all the land is borderland." This is "a postmodern landscape where Self and Other paw at the ghostly imaginings of each other's powers."[19]

It is worth keeping these histories of colonial mimicry in mind when looking at the so-called Indian Renaissance and the emergence of Indian nationalism that occurred in the late 1960s and '70s. Despite its many positive outcomes, certain strains of Indian nationalism have been particularly susceptible to the mimetic performance of authenticity that had been occurring for many decades. Acceptance of the category of race and the racialization of our identities is one example. These are ideas about identity that we inherited when we began to discuss our differences using the language of skin color—the "white man" and the "red man"—that define European racism.

In fact the most extreme nationalist positions appear the most assimilated when one is attentive to specific ideas and how they are articulated. Take the longstanding racist fear of miscegenation, which one hears articulated in our communities from time to time. In his 1995 autobiography, *Where White Men Fear to Tread*, activist-turned-actor Russell Means argues against intermarriage. He insists his position is based on the wisdom of his Lakota elders, but his language is borrowed directly from nineteenth- and early twentieth-century racist discourse.

Golden eagles don't mate with bald eagles, deer don't mate with antelope, gray wolves don't mate with red wolves. Just look at domesticated animals, at mongrel dogs, and mixed-breed horses, and you'll know the Great Mystery didn't intend them to be that way. We weakened the species and introduced disease by mixing what should be kept separate. Among humans, intermarriage weakens the respect people have for themselves and for their traditions. It undermines clarity of spirit and mind.[20]

Compare the structure and examples given in Means's argument to that of an earlier and more famous autobiographer:

Every animal mates only with a member of the same species. The titmouse seeks the titmouse, the finch the finch, the stork the stork, the fieldmouse the fieldmouse, the dourmouse the dourmouse, the wolf the she-wolf, etc.[21]

The latter writer is, of course, Adolf Hitler, writing about racial purity in *Mein Kampf*. Where white men fear to tread? Would that it were so. Walking in the footsteps of nineteenth-century European racists might have been a better title for this section of Means's book. The colossal categorical mistake that this argument is based on—conflating race with species—is so absurd that I don't feel obliged to refute it. I mention it here only to show the way in which European racism has been smuggled into some Indian nationalism, in this case adopted wholesale precisely where an "authentic" Indian identity is claimed to be most protected and pure. Of course Means's racism is fundamentally different from the National Socialist variety because he is not in much of a position to impose his ideas on others; my point here is not to draw a moral equivalency but to demonstrate that these are not our ideas in the first place, that we can only claim them from a space that is already complexly and deeply hybrid.

One could make a similar assertion about the concept of "blood memory," which has been circulating in discussions of indigenous culture since the 1960s with little sign of going away. According to the literary critic Chadwick Allen, this term was coined by the novelist N. Scott Momaday in his 1969 Pulitzer Prize–winning novel, *House Made of Dawn*. In fact, the phrase had been in use amongst racist ideologues since the Nazi era and remains in common use amongst right-wing racist groups up to the present. In Momaday's novel, the concept functioned to reconnect the author and his characters to a traditional Kiowa past from which he had become estranged: cultural memories that seemed lost, he decided, were in fact carried in the blood. Allen sees this move as "an obvious appropriation and redeployment of the U.S. government's attempt to systematize and regulate Indian identities through the tabulation of blood quantum."[22] It is an appropriation, to be sure, but I'm not convinced that it is much of a redeployment, since it retains the nineteenth-century racist insistence that character traits (and even relatively recent memory) can be inherited as racial characteristics. Allen is somewhat taken aback by the critic Arnold

Krupat's objection to the idea as being fundamentally racist. He ascribes this to "post Holocaust anxiety of fixed racial or 'blood' categories."[23] Well, yes, but another way to say the same thing is: "It is a bad thing to draw on Nazi ideas when you talk about race." Just as importantly, Allen's sense that this is the result of an implied oversensitivity to Nazi anti-Jewish racism misses the point that the Nazis did not invent the racist idea that character is carried in the blood, but rather, inherited it amongst a set of racist ideas that developed in Europe and America as the justifications for slavery, European colonization, and American manifest destiny expansionism.[24] We have as much historical reason to be "anxious" about the term as anyone.

As Allen notes, one of the ways that blood memory functions is as an absolute resistance to the appropriation of indigenous cultures. One can argue that, according to blood memory, a particular cultural concept might be an "Indian thing" that others are biologically incapable of understanding. Allen suggests that "the argument over blood memory has become an argument over potential and potentially irreconcilable disparities between Indian and non-Indian categories of truth."[25] I'm not sure what a "category of truth" is—perhaps an epistemic principle—but I believe that I have already given plenty of evidence that the ownership of the concept of blood memory cannot be divided into such a tidy binary division, that it is not drawn from a discrete indigenous episteme. As much as I understand the desire to imaginatively reconnect with traditional ideas from which we have become traumatically separated, why root this process in the "blood"—that is, the race—of those involved? Ascribing a supernatural dimension to the process is one element, but why did Momaday's blood memory provide him with a term for the process that is not derived from Kiowa thought but from the language of nineteenth-century racists? I believe that when you write in English and are immersed in the ideas that are built into its vocabularies, then you speak its ideas, even (perhaps especially) when you are attempting to say something "essential" about your supposed biological alterity.

The enforcement of a colonial idea of authenticity became codified for visual artists through the U.S. Indian Arts and Crafts Act of 1990, which was signed into law on November 29 by President George H. W. Bush. The Act was promoted as a means to prevent tourist kitsch made by non-Indians from being sold as Indian art or craft. The Act made it a criminal offence for a person or institution to suggest a product was of Native American origin unless the maker was an enrolled member of a federally recognized tribe. According to the Department of the Interior's Indian Arts and Crafts Board website it is a "truth-in-advertising law," which is an odd concept, particularly when it comes to the issue of cultural identity. How likely is it that "advertising" would be the arena in which such elusive "truths" are capable of being parsed? The penalties outlined by the Department of the Interior are nevertheless severe:

> For a first time violation of the Act, an individual can face civil or criminal penalties up to a $250,000 fine or a five-year prison term, or both. If a business violates the Act, it can face civil penalties or can be prosecuted and fined up to $1,000,000.[26]

The same webpage has a sidebar link labeled "To Report a Violation." Here the consumer is warned of the perils of advertising fake Indian Arts and Crafts as authentic:

> While the beauty, quality, and collectability of authentic Indian arts and crafts make each piece a unique reflection of our American heritage, it is important that buyers be aware that fraudulent Indian arts and crafts compete daily with authentic Indian arts and crafts in the nationwide marketplace. This consumer fraud not only harms the buyers, [but] also erodes the overall Indian arts and crafts market and the economic and cultural livelihood of Indian artists, craftspeople, and Tribes.[27]

This paragraph is informative in its assumptions about authenticity, its focus on "protecting" the nonindigenous consumer, and its patronizing tone. The Indian "Tribes" and their art are subsumed within "our" (America's) "heritage" of which they are a "reflection." Reflection is exactly the right word—the creation of such crafts is a reflection, in perfect imitation, of America's desire for quaint Indians whose art is, of course, part of America's past, its "heritage" rather than its present or future. It is fixed and stable and open for consumption, its value and meaning guaranteed in advance by its authenticity, which allows the consumer the special privilege of not having to know enough about traditional indigenous arts or culture to tell the difference between a plastic "made in Taiwan" knockoff and the "real thing." Despite the support of some indigenous artists, I suspect that the law was enacted less out of sympathy for indigenous peoples than to preserve the mythology of authenticity that drives a fortune in tourist dollars to locations associated with indigenous arts and crafts, particularly in the American Southwest.

The Act has been critiqued from a number of different positions, including those that argue convincingly about the ludicrous ways that one might or might not end up an enrolled member of a particular tribe (including in many cases the racist standard of blood-quantum).[28] But my interest in the context of this essay is on the idea that possession of a state-recognized Indian identity is somehow a guarantee of cultural authenticity. Last year a student gave me the gift of a small, framed artwork. On the back is a "Certificate of Authenticity" providing the artist's name, photograph, registration number, and text about "authentic Navajo sandpaintings," of which, one presumes, this is meant to be an example. Of course there has been controversy within Diné (Navajo) communities about fixing the traditionally transient sand-painted images by adhering them to glued surfaces and marketing them commercially when their original use was medicinal, but my objection to the "authenticity" of this work is less subtle. The image depicted in the work is the vanquished Indian from the sculpture *The End of the Trail*, by the white artist James Earle Fraser (1876–1973), a work notorious for being the quintessential expression of the trope of the vanishing Indian. The artist's "authenticity" doesn't guarantee the work's quality either; the horse and rider are depicted in silhouette, but the supposedly emaciated horse has a head with a profile more like that of the stuffed donkey Eeyore from the Disney cartoons than a warrior's mount. So much for truth in advertising.

Race may be skin deep, but colonial ideology stretches out for miles and penetrates everything. Our way out of this trap is not to think of our heritage as set in the blood and constantly in jeopardy of contamination, but as culture—not something we are obliged to mimetically reproduce, but rather, a tool box of strategies for being in the world from which we can actively and reflectively choose and develop.

Terrance Houle, *Urban Indian Series* (no. 7), 2007. Eight digital C-prints, 35.6 x 27.9 cm each. Collection of the artist. Photo by Jarusha Brown.

Sonya Kelliher-Combs

Born in Bethel, Alaska, in 1969 and raised in Nome, Sonya Kelliher-Combs (Inupiaq/
Athabascan) holds a bachelor of fine arts (1992) from the University of Alaska Fairbanks, and a master of fine arts (1998) from Arizona State University, Tempe. Her
artwork continually references a sense of place, history, culture, and family. Kelliher-
Combs is the recipient of numerous awards, including the Eiteljorg Museum Fellowship, the Anchorage, Alaska, Mayor's Individual Artist Award, the Arctic Education
Foundation Academic Excellence Award, and the Best of Show honor at the *Vision
of New Eyes* exhibition, Visual Arts Center of Alaska, Anchorage.

UNTITLED
wearing trim
a crest, a clan, an identifier
who you are

a pore
sifting, shifting
catching, releasing
pouring

secrets
hiding, guarding
gathering
scraps
the stuff one does not talk about

the three that got away
cords of regret
a tie that cannot be cut
idiot strings

tattoo
marking, seaming
wearing, walking
passage

—Sonya Kelliher-Combs

SELECTED SOLO EXHIBITIONS

2008 *Walrus Family Portraits*, International Gallery of
Contemporary Art, Anchorage, AK

2007 *New Secrets*, Well Street Art Company, Fairbanks, AK

2006 *Unraveled Secrets*, Institute of American Indian Arts
Museum, Santa Fe, NM

2005 Solo Exhibition Series, Anchorage Museum of History
and Art, Anchorage, AK

2002 *1000 Secrets*, Decker/Morris Gallery, Anchorage, AK

2001 *Idiot Strings: Catch and Release*, Alaska State Museum,
Juneau, AK

2000 *New Works*, Bunnell Street Gallery, Homer, AK

1998 *Asianggataq*, Harry Wood Gallery, Arizona State
University, Tempe, AZ

1996 *In Search of Self*, Fort Lewis College, Durango, CO

1994 *Transformation*, University of Alaska Fine Arts Gallery, Fairbanks, AK

1990 Carrie M. McLain Memorial Museum, Nome, AK

SELECTED GROUP EXHIBITIONS

2009 *Dry Ice: Alaska Native Artists and the Landscape*, Paul Robeson Center for the Arts,
Princeton, NJ

2007 *Diversity and Dialogue: The Eiteljorg Fellowship for Native American Fine Art*, Eiteljorg
Museum of American Indians and Western Art, Indianapolis, IN

2005 *Changing Hands: Art Without Reservation 2*, Museum of Arts and Design, New York, NY
Cheongju International Craft Biennial, Cheongju Arts Center, Cheongju, South Korea

2004 *Alaska Native Art: People of a Place, Art of a People*, Sotheby's Institute of Art, New York, NY

2003 *Points of View*, Anchorage Museum of History and Art, Anchorage, AK

2001 *State of the Art Biennial*, Parkland College Art Gallery, Champaign, IL

2000 *Convergence: The Exhibition of the 2000 Arctic Winter Games*, Yukon Arts Centre,
Whitehorse, YT

1997 *Painting Is Dead, Long Live Painting*, Memorial Union, Arizona State University, Tempe, AZ

1995 First Peoples Gallery, New York, NY

1993 *Arts from the Arctic*, Anchorage Museum of History and Art, Anchorage, AK

1992 Institute of Alaska Native Arts, Fairbanks, AK

SELECTED COLLECTIONS

Alaska State Museum, Juneau, AK

Anchorage Museum of History and Art, Anchorage, AK

Anchorage School District, Chugiak High School, Chugiak, AK

Anchorage School District, South Anchorage High School, Anchorage AK

Eiteljorg Museum of American Indians and Western Art, Indianapolis IN

Fairbanks International Airport, Fairbanks, AK

Ted Stevens International Airport, Anchorage, AK

University of Alaska Museum of the North, Fairbanks, AK

Nadia Myre

www.nadiamyre.com

Multidisciplinary artist Nadia Myre (Anishinaabe) was born in 1974 and is currently living and working in Montreal, Canada. Myre earned fine arts degrees from Camosun College in Victoria, British Columbia, and the Emily Carr University of Art and Design in Vancouver, British Columbia. In 2002 she obtained a master of fine arts from Concordia University in Montreal, Quebec. Her work, which has been shown in Canada and abroad, has received honored recognition from the Canada Council for the Arts, the Conseil des arts et des lettres du Québec, the National Aboriginal Achievement Foundation, and an Eiteljorg Fellowship for Native American Fine Art.

My work is about desire.

For over a decade, I have explored notions of longing and loss, as well as the incessant human drive to reconcile the two—and perhaps heal in some way. Yet whether it is through some kind of reckoning; or a blissful union where recrimination, pain, and reproof are absent; or the body is physically thrown into extreme states to absolve, abolish, or numb this drive—still longing lingers.

For me, this desire is manifold and stems from the myriad stories I live or come across—the desire for land, for another, for language, for the end of dissonance between languages, for the union of two cultures, but strongest of all (as longing is the thread that binds us to this world) is for desire itself to remain.

SELECTED SOLO EXHIBITIONS

2009 *Landscape of Sorrow and other new work*, Art Mûr, Montreal, QC

2008 *Othered Women*, The Red Shift Gallery, Saskatoon, SK

 Nadia Myre: Works on Paper, St. Francis Xavier University Art Gallery, Antigonish, NS

 A fleur de peau, Musée d'art contemporain des Laurentides, St.-Jérôme, QC

2007 *The Scar Project*, Urban Shaman Gallery, Winnipeg, MB

2006 *Want Ads and Other Scars*, Urban Shaman Gallery, Winnipeg, MB

2005 *Skin Deep, or Poetry for the Blind*, Union Gallery, Queen's University, Kingston, ON

2004 *Cicatrices, ou poésie pour les aveugles*, Art Mûr, Montreal, QC

2002 *Indian Act*, Grunt Gallery, Vancouver, BC

 Cont[r]act, Galerie Oboro, Montreal, QC

2001 *Riding Lines*, Indian Art Centre, Hull, QC

SELECTED GROUP EXHIBITIONS

2009 *Remix: New Modernities in a Post-Indian World*, Art Gallery of Ontario; George Gustav Heye Center, National Museum of the American Indian, New York, NY (2008); Heard Museum, Phoenix, AZ (2007)

2008 *Never let the facts get in the way of the truth*, Western Front, Vancouver, BC

2006 *Making Sense of Things*, McMaster Museum of Art, McMaster University, Hamilton, ON; C. N. Gorman Museum, University of California, Davis, CA

2005 *The American West*, Compton Verney Gallery, London, England

2004 *Unfolding Territories*, Faculty of Creative Arts Gallery, University of Wollongong, New South Wales, Australia, and Flinders University, Adelaide, Australia

2003 *Path Breakers: The Eiteljorg Fellowship for Native American Fine Art*, Eiteljorg Museum of American Indians and Western Art, Indianapolis, IN

2002 *Animate Objects*, Sâkêwêwak Artists' Collective, Regina, SK

1999 *Uh...Ummmm...Ahh...Stop*, Montréal Telegraph Gallery, Montreal, QC

1998 *Here and Now: First Peoples Perspective 1964-1997*, Emily Carr University of Art and Design, Vancouver, BC

1996 *Wild Women Revue*, Wilna Thomas Cultural Centre, Camosun College, Victoria, BC; En'owkin Centre, Penticton, BC; Malaspina College, Duncan, BC

SELECTED COLLECTIONS

Canada Council Art Bank, Ottawa, ON

Canadian Museum of Civilization, Gatineau, QC

Eiteljorg Museum of Indians and Western Art, Indianapolis, IN

Art Mûr, Montreal, QC

MacKenzie Art Gallery, Regina, SK

Musée National des Beaux-Arts du Québec, QC

National Aboriginal Achievement Foundation, Toronto, ON

Urban Shaman Gallery, Winnipeg, MB

Woodland Cultural Centre, Brantford, ON

Michael Belmore

Michael Belmore (Ojibway), a member of the Royal Canadian Academy of Arts, was born in 1971 north of Thunder Bay, Ontario. He holds an associated diploma (1994) in sculpture/installation from the Ontario College of Art and Design in Toronto and currently lives in the Haliburton Highlands in Ontario. Belmore works in a variety of media including plastics, metal, wood, and stone. These materials are important to understanding his work, which looks at how we view nature as a commodity. Belmore's work has earned numerous awards from the Ontario Arts Council, the Canada Council for the Arts, and the Canadian Native Arts Foundation.

The North American landscape, especially its watersheds, continues to be shaped by our divergent tendencies to that of nature. Rivers have been dammed, streams redirected, and wetlands drained, all in order to better satisfy the demands of Western society. Over the past few years my practice has focused primarily on stone carving and the traditional metalsmithing technique of chasing and repoussé. Through the arduous process of hammering copper, I have continued to map out waterways through calculated and miscalculated blows. The shorelines of New York City offer the perfect opportunity to demonstrate fully our long influencing actions on landscape. Although this work is not literally in skin, as landscape and as place it is just as much a part of us.

SELECTED SOLO EXHIBITIONS

2009 *Embankment*, Station Gallery, Whitby, ON

2006 *Downstream*, Forest City Gallery, London, ON

2005 *Stream*, Rails End Gallery and Arts Centre, Haliburton, ON

2002 *Vantage Point*, Sacred Circle Gallery of American Indian Art, Seattle, WA

2001 *fly by wire*, AKA Artist-Run Centre/Tribe, Saskatoon, SK

2000 *Eating Crow*, Sâkêwêwak Artists' Collective, Regina, SK

1999 *Ravens Wait*, Indian Art Centre, Hull, QC

SELECTED GROUP EXHIBITIONS

2008 *Scout's Honour*, University of Lethbridge Art Gallery, Lethbridge, AB; Urban Shaman Gallery, Winnipeg, MB; Museum London, London, ON

2007 *Terra Incognita*, Macdonald Stewart Art Centre, Guelph, ON

2006 *Nuit Blanche*, Spin Gallery, Toronto, ON

2005 *...the beast not found in verse*, McMaster Museum of Art, McMaster University, Hamilton, ON

2004 *Three Rivers: wild waters, sacred places*, Yukon Arts Centre, Whitehorse, YT; The Robert McLaughlin Gallery, Oshawa, ON; Maltwood Art Museum and Gallery, University of Victoria, BC; Kelowna Art Gallery, Kelowna, BC; Art Gallery of Peterborough, Peterborough, ON; Whyte Museum of the Canadian Rockies, Banff, AB

2003 *Light Conditions*, Agnes Etherington Art Centre, Kingston, ON

2002 *Gridlock*, York Quay Gallery, Harbourfront Centre, Toronto, ON

2001 *Transition 2: Contemporary Indian and Inuit Art of Canada*, Gallery 418, Montreal, QC; Yukon Arts Centre, Whitehorse, YT

2000 *Beaver Tales*, Oakville Galleries, Oakville, ON

1999 *Wolves in the City*, Edmonton Art Gallery, Edmonton, AB

SELECTED COLLECTIONS

Agnes Etherington Art Centre, Queen's University, Kingston, ON

Art Gallery of Peterborough, Peterborough, ON

Indian and Inuit Art Centre, Indian and Northern Affairs Canada, Gatineau, QC

McMichael Canadian Art Collection, Kleinburg, ON

Macdonald Stewart Art Centre, Guelph, ON

Thunder Bay Art Gallery, Thunder Bay, ON

KC Adams

www.kcadams.net

Born in 1971, the Winnipeg-based artist KC Adams (Métis) earned a bachelor of fine arts from Concordia University in Montréal and has focused her work on the investigation of the relationship between nature (the living) and technology (progress). She has received several grants and awards from the Winnipeg Arts Council, Manitoba Arts Council, and Canada Council for the Arts, and twenty pieces from her *Cyborg Hybrid* series are in the permanent collection of the National Art Gallery in Ottawa. Adams was the director of the Urban Shaman Gallery in Winnipeg from 2008 to 2009. She currently lives and works in Winnipeg.

Cyborg Hybrids *attempts to challenge our views toward mixed-race classifications by using humorous text and imagery from two cultures. The* Cyborg Hybrids *are digital prints of Euro-Aboriginal artists who are forward thinkers and plugged in with technology. They follow the doctrine of Donna Haraway's* Cyborg Manifesto, *which states that a cyborg is a creature in a technological, postgender world, free of traditional Western stereotypes towards race and gender. I photograph artists who fit the* Cyborg Hybrid *criteria and have them wear white T-shirts with beaded text representing slogans that illustrate common phrases that stereotype aboriginal people. I also create white chokers for them to wear while I photograph them in stoic poses, mocking photographs of aboriginal people from the nineteenth and early twentieth centuries. I then digitally alter the photos to make them look like they could fit within a glamorous magazine. The defiant poses of the subjects challenge the viewer to try and classify their identities.*

KC Adams, *Cyborg Hybrid Alli* (left),
and *Cyborg Hybrid Teresa*, 2009.
Digital print, 50.8 x 35.6 cm each.
Collection of the artist.

SELECTED SOLO EXHIBITIONS

2008   *Cyborg Hybrids*, Odd Gallery, Dawson City, YT

2006   *Cyborg Hybrids (Banff & Winnipeg Series)*, National Gallery of Canada, Ottawa, ON

2005   *Cyborg Living*, The Annex, Winnipeg, MB

2004   *Bleach Series: Cyborgs & Hybrids*, The Other Gallery, Banff, MB

2000   *Antithesis: Nature and Technology*, Urban Shaman Gallery, Winnipeg, MB

SELECTED GROUP EXHIBITIONS

2008   *Anthem: Perspectives on Home and Native Land*, Mount Saint Vincent University Art
Gallery, Halifax, NS; Walter Phillips Gallery, Banff, AB; Carleton University, High
and Main Gallery, Ottawa, ON

2008   *Steeling the Gaze: Portraits by Aboriginal Artists*, Canadian Museum of Contemporary
Photography at the National Gallery of Canada, Ottawa, ON

2007   *Photoquai: biennale des images du monde, 1ère édition*, Musée du quai Branly, Paris, France

2005   *The Language of Intercession*, OBORO Gallery, Montreal, QC

2004   *Last Winnipeg Annual*, The Annex, Winnipeg, MB

2003   *Slap & Tickle*, Urban Shaman Gallery, Winnipeg, MB

2001   *Group Show*, The Other Gallery, Banff Centre for the Arts, Winnipeg, MB

1999   *World Tea Party*, Plug In Institute of Contemporary Art, Winnipeg, MB

SELECTED COLLECTIONS

Concordia University Centre for Native Education, Montreal, QC

Manitoba Arts Council Art Bank, Winnipeg, MB

National Gallery of Canada, Ottawa, ON

University of Manitoba, Winnipeg, MB

Winnipeg Art Gallery, Winnipeg, MB

Rosalie Favell

Rosalie Favell (Cree Métis) is a photo-based artist. Born in 1958, she was raised in Winnipeg, Manitoba. A graduate of Ryerson Polytechnic Institute in Toronto (bachelor of applied arts, 1984), Favell holds a master of fine arts (1998) from the University of New Mexico in Albuquerque. She has extensive teaching experience at the postgraduate level and is currently completing a PhD at Carleton University in Ottawa. Favell has received several awards, including the Ontario Arts Council Chalmers Arts Fellowship and the Canada Council for the Arts Victor Martyn Lynch-Staunton Award.

Facing the Camera *is a document series on aboriginal artists, rooted in my desire to image my community. The work goes back to the beginnings of my career. When I first learned photography, I wanted to look at who I was; the color of my skin, as it was different from my mother's skin, was an important part of this investigation. In* Facing the Camera, *I have not tried to pose people. The images are meant to have an edge to them as people find some way of dealing with the camera. To be visualized is a way in which one acknowledges the construction of a positive or empowered representation that includes engaging with, at some level, the numerous social and cultural factors, both good and bad, Aboriginal and Western, that have affected an understanding of self. This idea of "self" is not necessarily linked to individualism. Rather, it can be seen as connected to communal needs and values, a sense of place and traditions, as well as personal and extended history. The challenge is to know your own part in this, to know your own place in the picture.*

Rosalie Favell, *Barry Ace* (left) and *Nadia Myre*, 2008 and 2009. From the *Facing the Camera* series, digital print, 61 x 50.8 cm each. Collection of the artist.

SELECTED SOLO EXHIBITIONS

2009   *Reveal*, The Ottawa Art Gallery, Ottawa, ON

2008   *Cultural Mediations*, Urban Shaman Gallery, Winnipeg, MB

2005   *Rosalie Favell*, Art Gallery of Algoma, Sault Ste. Marie, ON

2003   *Rosalie Favell: I Searched Many Worlds*, Winnipeg Art Gallery, Winnipeg, MB

2000   *Longing and Not Belonging*, Thunder Bay Art Gallery, Thunder Bay. ON; Kitchener-Waterloo Art Gallery, Kitchener, ON

1997   *"It was a moment…"* John Sommers Gallery, University of New Mexico, Albuquerque, NM

1995   *Living Evidence*, Fotofeis '95, International Festival of Photography, Edinburgh, Scotland

1993   *Portraits in Blood*, Native Indian/Inuit Photographers' Association Gallery, Hamilton, ON

SELECTED GROUP EXHIBITIONS

2009   *Home/land and Security*, Render Gallery, University of Waterloo, Waterloo, ON

2008   *Steeling the Gaze: Portraits by Aboriginal Artists*, Canadian Museum of Contemporary Photography at the National Gallery of Canada, Ottawa, ON

2006   *Our People, Our Land, Our Images*, C. N. Gorman Museum, University of California at Davis, Davis, CA

2005   *About Face: Self-Portraits by Native American and First Nations Artists*, Wheelwright Museum of the American Indian, Santa Fe, NM

2004   *Gatherings: Aboriginal Art from the Collection of the Winnipeg Art Gallery*, Guangdong Museum of Art, Guangzhou, China

2002   *Cross Generational*, North Dakota Museum of Art, Grand Forks, ND

2000   *alt.shift.control: Musings on Digital Identity*, Art Gallery of Hamilton, Hamilton, ON

1999   *Emergence from the Shadows: First Peoples' Photographic Perspectives*, Canadian Museum of Civilization, Hull, QC

1998   *Exploring Old Territory in a New Way: A Group Exhibition of Native North American Artists*, Rathbone Gallery, The Sage Colleges, Albany Campus, Albany, NY

1996   *Positives and Negatives: Native American Photographers*, Westfälisches Landesmuseum für Kunst und Kulturgeschichte, Munster, Germany

1994   *Traditions of Looking*, Institute of American Indian Arts Museum, Santa Fe, NM

SELECTED COLLECTIONS

Canadian Museum of Contemporary Photography at the National Gallery of Canada, Ottawa, ON

Indian and Inuit Art Centre, Indian and Northern Affairs, Gatineau, QC

Manitoba Arts Council Art Bank, Winnipeg, MB

Mount Saint Vincent University, Halifax, NS

Rockwell Museum of Western Art, Corning, NY

Smithsonian's National Museum of the American Indian, Washington, DC

Winnipeg Art Gallery, Winnipeg, MB

Woodland Cultural Centre, Brantford, ON

Terrance Houle

www.terrancehoule.com

Terrance Houle (Blood) was born in 1975, resides in Calgary, Alberta, and holds a bachelor of fine arts (2003) from Alberta College of Art and Design. Houle's artwork utilizes performance, photography, video/film, music, and painting, as well as tools of mass dissemination such as billboards and vinyl bus signage. Houle has received numerous awards, including an invitation to participate in the 2003 Thematic Residency at the Banff Centre for the Arts, the Best Experimental Film award at the Toronto 2004 ImagineNATIVE Film and Media Arts Festival, and the 2006 Enbridge Emerging Artist Award.

The Urban Indian Series *is a comment on personal identity and cultural commodity in today's contemporary culture. Specifically, what is my culture as it compares to the mainstream understanding of Native Peoples? My regalia is both a catalyst in the image, breaking up the sea of mundane Western garb, and a representation that is part of my everyday, much like my culture, thus challenging the suggestion that I am out of place in a world that only identifies with conformity. The work serves to question ideas of tradition, identity, and culture that are often negated or replaced by Western cultural standards. Also, in capturing the image of the "Indian" in portraiture and regalia, the* Urban Indian Series *seeks to comment on the historical relationship between photography and Aboriginal identity.*

Terrance Houle, *Urban Indian Series* (no. 8), 2007. Eight digital C-prints, 35.6 x 27.9 cm each. Collection of the artist. Photo by Jarusha Brown.

SELECTED SOLO EXHIBITIONS

2008 *85.11.16*, SKEW Gallery, Calgary, AB

2005 *Remember In Grade…*, +15 Window Project, The New Gallery, Calgary, AB

Kipi-Dapi-Pook-Aki, Taking Back Control, Glenbow Museum, Calgary, AB

2002 *A Little Western*, +15 Window Project, Truck Gallery, Calgary, AB

SELECTED GROUP EXHIBITIONS

2008 *Through the Looking Glass*, Glenbow Museum, Calgary, AB

Face the Nation, Art Gallery of Alberta, Edmonton, AB

Photo LA 2008, SKEW Gallery, Los Angeles, CA

2007 *Photo Miami 2007*, SKEW Gallery, Miami, FL

The World Upside Down, Agnes Etherington Art Centre, Kingston, ON

2006 *Red Eye*, Carleton University Art Gallery, Ottawa, ON

The Bodies That Were Not Ours, Linden-St. Kilda Centre for the Contemporary Arts, St. Kilda, Victoria, Australia

2005 *Electrofringe Festival, This Is Not Art Festival*, Field Contemporary Art Space, Newcastle, New South Wales, Australia

The American West, Compton Verney Gallery, Warwickshire, England

2004 *Out of the Dark*, wiseART Gallery, Brisbane, Australia

Indian. Unquote, Roundhouse Community Arts and Recreation Centre, Vancouver, BC

2003 *Turtle Island*, The Other Gallery, Banff Centre for the Arts, AB

SELECTED COLLECTIONS

Alberta Foundation for the Arts, Edmonton, AB

Calgary Arts Collection, Calgary, AB

Glenbow Museum, Calgary, AB

National Archives of Canada, Ottawa, ON

Arthur Renwick

Photo-based artist Arthur Renwick (Haisla) was born in Kitimat, British Columbia, in 1965, received fine arts degrees from both Vancouver Community College (1986) and Emily Carr University of Art and Design (1989) in Vancouver, and his master of fine arts from Concordia University in Montreal (1993). Renwick creates thoughtfully crafted works that combine photography with wood, aluminum, and copper. In addition to having received numerous Ontario Arts Council and Canada Council awards, Renwick won the K. M. Hunter Artist Award in 2005.

The portrait series Mask *is a departure from my previous work in multimedia landscape photography. These large color prints document First Nations people who have come up against cultural assumptions about their heritage throughout their careers. Whether they are archaeologists like Michael White, hired to excavate bones in a suburban residential development, or actors like Fernando Hernandez, who played a Mayan shaman in Mel Gibson's film* Apocalypto, *they have all had to combat prevailing stereotypes in order to establish and retain their own identity. During the portrait sittings for* Mask, *I initiated a dialogue with my subjects, seeking their thoughts on the notion of identity. To undermine historic Indian portraiture, I invited the sitters to look into the lens and make a facial gesture. The results are fresh and often startling images that are neither stoic nor noble.*

Arthur Renwick, *Thomas*, 2006. Digital print (ed. 3/3), 119.4 x 114.3 cm. Collection of the artist.

SELECTED SOLO EXHIBITIONS

2009   *Mask: Artists and Curators*, Leo Kamen Gallery, Toronto, ON

2008   *Delegates: Chiefs of the Earth and Sky*, aneco, Saskatoon, SK; National Museum of Brasília, Brazil

2007   *Arthur Renwick: First Nations Churches in British Columbia* in conjunction with the AGO exhibition *Emily Carr: New Perspectives on a Canadian Icon; And the word was...*, Art Gallery of Ontario, Toronto, ON

2006   *Mask*, Leo Kamen Gallery, Toronto, ON

2005   *Delegates: Chiefs of the Earth and Sky*, Le Mois de la Photo à Montréal, Montreal, QC; Urban Shaman Gallery, Winnipeg, MB; Leo Kamen Gallery, Toronto, ON

2004   *Totem Hysteria*, The Photo Passage, Harbourfront Centre, Toronto, ON

2002   *Stately Monuments*, Gallery 44 Centre for Contemporary Photography, Toronto, ON

2001   *Overburden: askihk pehtakosiw = a voice is heard in the earth*, Keyano College Art Gallery, Fort McMurray, AB

SELECTED GROUP EXHIBITIONS

2009   *Steeling the Gaze: Portraits by Aboriginal Artists*, Canadian Museum of Contemporary Photography at the National Gallery of Canada, Ottawa, ON

2008   *Comic Relief*, National Gallery of Canada, Ottawa, ON
Bad Dog, No Biscuit!, Leo Kamen Gallery, Toronto, ON
Izhizkawe: To Leave Tracks to a Certain Place, FOFA Gallery, Concordia University, Montreal, QC

2007   *Confluence: First Nations Art*, Carleton University, Ottawa, ON
Dancing Through Time II, MacLaren Art Centre, Barrie, ON
Re/Translation: Land and Language, A Space Gallery, Toronto, ON

2006   *Faking Death*, Jack Shainman Gallery, New York, NY

2004   *First Nation's Art 2004*, Woodland Cultural Centre, Brantford, ON

2003   *Dig/Dug*, Koffler Gallery, Toronto, ON

2002   *Cool Stuff*, Summer Group Show, Leo Kamen Gallery, Toronto, ON
Indian Art/Facts, George Eastman House, International Museum of Photography and Film, Rochester, NY

2001   *Multiples: Tsa de yoh don's*, Walter Phillips Gallery, The Banff Centre, Banff, AB

2000   *Dust on the Road*, York Quay Gallery, Toronto, ON

1999   *FELT: Material Explorations*, Textile Museum of Canada, Toronto, ON
Re:Collections—First Nations Photographers, Winnipeg Art Gallery, MB

1998   *Here and Now: First Nations Alumni Art Exhibition*, Concourse Art Gallery, Emily Carr Institute of Art and Design, Vancouver, BC

1996   *Dis/location Markers*, Gallery TPW, Toronto; Art Gallery of Windsor, Windsor, ON

1994   *Nation to Nation*, Centre d'histoire de Montréal, Montreal, QC

1993   *Multiplicity: A New Cultural Strategy*, Museum of Anthropology at the University of British Columbia, Vancouver, BC

1991   *Strengthening the Spirit*, National Gallery of Canada, Ottawa, ON

SELECTED COLLECTIONS

Art Gallery of Hamilton, Hamilton, ON
Canada Council Art Bank, Ottawa, ON
Canadian Museum of Civilization, Gatineau, QC
Carleton University Art Gallery, Carleton University, Ottawa, ON
Indian and Inuit Art Centre, Department of Indian and Northern Affairs, Gatineau, QC
National Gallery of Canada, Ottawa, ON
Winnipeg Art Gallery, Winnipeg, MB
Woodland Cultural Centre, Brantford, ON

Sarah Sense

www.sarahsense.com

Sarah Sense (Chitimacha/Choctaw) was born in 1980 and raised in a suburb of
Sacramento, California. Sense received a bachelor of fine arts (2003) from California
State University, Chico, and a master of fine arts (2005) from Parsons, The New
School for Design in New York City. Sense has worked as an administrator, curator,
project director, and educator at various art institutions, including the American
Indian Community House Gallery in New York City, the Hammer Museum at the
University of California, Los Angeles, and the Institute of American Indian Arts in
Santa Fe, New Mexico. She is a practicing artist and muralist, and has completed
four murals in Louisiana and California. Currently, Sense is living and working
in California.

KARL

*Explorations of ancestry through familial archives have uncovered
ironic reflections of the complexities of communities, ethnicities,
and aesthetics within the United States. My works weave cultural
representations of realities and myths into stable patterns replicating
mathematics and the moments when logic falls apart. The missing
spaces echo the glitches in binary codes and their constructs.*

*"There are a couple of publications of mine that are missing.
I can't find them." Aesthetic changes occur when the pattern is
affected by numerical sequences shifting from a language of tradition to one of science. The transition moves from a Native ancestry
of one grandfather into a German archive of another grandfather
through the commonality of their aerospace careers in the United
States. A psychological marriage thus develops between these men
in the space that is missing.*

*It's not about being Native. It's not about being German.
It's about uncanny circumstances that are beyond our control yet
important to recognize because they make up who we are.*

SELECTED SOLO EXHIBITIONS

2008   *New Work by Sarah Sense*, Blue Rain Gallery, Santa Fe, NM

2005   *Sarah Sense*, MTV/Viacom, New York, NY

2002   *Constructs*, BFA Solo Exhibition, California State University, Chico, CA

SELECTED GROUP EXHIBITIONS

2010   *Beyond Myths: Native American Realities*, Kidspace gallery at MASS MoCA,
        North Adams, MA
        Vision: Rick Bartow, Sarah Sense, and Hoka Skenandore, Berlin Gallery, Heard Museum,
        Phoenix AZ

2009   *Cultural Myths*, Albuquerque Film Festival, Albuquerque, NM
        spctclr vws, Brooklyn, NY
        Outsiders Within, Tempe Center for the Arts, Tempe, AZ
        New Directions, Berlin Gallery, Phoenix, AZ

2008   *HOW: Engagements with the Hollywood Indian*, A Space Gallery, Toronto, ON
        Redefining Native Traditions, Blue Rain Gallery, Santa Fe, NM

2007   *VIEW THREE*, Nicole Fiacco Gallery, Hudson, NY

2006   *Paumanok*, State University of New York, Stony Brook, NY

2005   *Art Parade*, Deitch Projects, New York, NY
        New York Mix: Five Civilized Boroughs, American Indian Community House Gallery,
        New York, NY

COLLECTIONS

Private collections in the United States and Canada

Notes

ASH-MILBY

1. J. M. Barrie, *Peter and Wendy* (London: Hodder & Stoughton, 1911), 64 (online).

2. See the repartee between Spokane/Coeur d'Alene author Sherman Alexie and humorist Stephen Colbert on p. 79 (*The Colbert Report,* October 28, 2008) in which the use of the term "skins" and its sensitivity are demonstrated.

3. Ives Goddard, "'I am a Red-Skin': The Adoption of a Native American Expression (1769–1826)," *European Review of Native American Studies* 19, no. 2 (2005): 1–20.

4. See Carol Spindel, *Dancing at Halftime: Sports and the Controversy over American Indian Mascots* (New York: New York University Press, 2000); C. Richard King and Charles Fruehling Springwood, eds., *Team Spirits: The Native American Mascots Controversy* (Lincoln and London: University of Nebraska Press, 2001).

5. *Suzan Shown Harjo et al. v. Pro-Football, Inc.,* filed in 1992. Spokane activist and artist Charlene Teters has been particularly outspoken about this issue. See her website for numerous links to more information: www.charleneteters.com.

6. Jason Lujan, artist statement, 2009. www.jasonlujan.com.

7. Sonia Katyal, "Semiotic Disobedience," *Washington University Law Review* 84, no. 2 (2006): 511–12.

8. See Robert E. Bieder, *Science Encounters the Indian, 1820–1880: The Early Years of American Ethnology* (Norman: University of Oklahoma Press, 1986), 1–12.

9. Orin Starn, *Ishi's Brain: In Search of America's Last 'Wild' Indian* (New York: Norton, 2004).

10. Kenn Harper, *Give Me My Father's Body: The Life of Minik, the New York Eskimo* (South Royalton, VT: Steerforth Press, 2000).

11. *Bodies Revealed* was first exhibited in 2004; *Bodies . . . The Exhibition* began touring in 2005. Both are ongoing, toured by Premier Exhibitions, Inc., based in Atlanta, GA.

12. Elaine Catz, "Sunday Forum: Exhibition of Exploitation, *Pittsburgh Post-Gazette* (online), June 24, 2007.

13. Ironically, Gunther von Hagens, the inventor of the plastination process and the organizer of the first exhibition of this kind, *Body Worlds* (1995–present),

has always been meticulous about procuring specimens through a body-donation program for which he receives consent prior to the donor's death.

14. Pauline Wakeham, *Taxidermic Signs: Reconstructing Aboriginality* (Minneapolis: University of Minnesota Press, 2008), 25.

15. Ibid., 5.

16. Sonya Kelliher-Combs, personal communication with the author, September 2009.

17. For images of this work, see Patricia Deadman, *Terra Incognita: Mary Anne Barkhouse and Michael Belmore* (Guelph, ON: Macdonald Stewart Art Centre, 2007).

18. For a more detailed description of *Upland* and the location, see Sally McKay, "Relatively Remote: The Tree Museum's Decade in the Woods," *Canadian Art* (Summer 2008), 75.

19. Edward S. Casey, *Earth-Mapping: Artists Reshaping Landscape* (Minneapolis: University of Minnesota Press, 2005), xv.

20. See Lucy Lippard, ed., *Partial Recall: With Essays on Photographs of Native North Americans* (New York: New Press, 1992); *Strong Hearts: Native American Visions and Voices* (New York: Aperture, 1995); Theresa Harlan, "Adjusting the Focus to an Indigenous Presence," in *Over Exposed: Essays on Contemporary Photography*, Carol Squiers, ed. (New York: New Press, 1999); Hulleah J. Tsinhnahjinnie and Veronica Passalacqua, eds., *Our People, Our Land, Our Images: International Indigenous Photographers* (Berkeley: Heyday Books, 2007).

21. C. Jill O'Bryan, *Carnal Art: Orlan's Refacing* (Minneapolis: University of Minnesota Press, 2005), 89.

22. Donna Haraway, "A Manifesto for Cyborgs: Science, Technology, and Socialist Feminism in the 1980s," rev. reprint in *The Uncanny: Experiments in Cyborg Culture*, ed. Bruce Grenville (Vancouver: Vancouver Art Gallery in partnership with Arsenal Pulp Press, 2001), 139.

23. Ryan Rice, *Anthem: Perspectives on Home and Native Land* (Ottawa, Ontario: Carleton University Art Gallery, 2007), 18–19.

24. Philip J. Deloria, *Indians in Unexpected Places* (Lawrence: University Press of Kansas, 2004), 4–5.

RINGLERO

1. Sonya Kelliher-Combs, conversations and correspondence with the author, 2009. The author sincerely thanks Ms. Kelliher- Combs for many hours spent discussing her art in preparation for this exhibition, and for the generous "care packages" from Anchorage.

2. See Bill Holm, *Northwest Coast Indian Art: An Analysis of Form* (Seattle: University of Washington Press, 1965).

3. Kelliher-Combs to the author, 2009.

4. Ibid.

5. Kelliher-Combs, conversation with author, March 2009.

6. Julie Decker, "Guarded Secrets: The Art of Sonya Kelliher-Combs," *American Indian Art Magazine* 33, no. 1 (Winter 2007), 61.

7. Decker, "Guarded Secrets," 62.

8. Bruce Bernstein, "It's Art: Keep Talking While We Keep Working But Hold It Down So I Can Hear Myself Think," in *Changing Hands: Art Without Reservation 2*, ed. David Revere McFadden and Ellen Napiura Taubman (New York: Museum of Arts and Design, 2005), 177.

9. See analysis of the "echo" identified in Sandy Gillespie, "Sonya Kelliher-Combs: Secrets," in *Diversity and Dialogue: The Eiteljorg Fellowship for Native American Fine Art*, 2007, ed. James H. Nottage (Indianapolis: Eiteljorg Museum of American Indians and Western Art; Seattle: University of Washington Press, 2008), 60–75.

10. Sonya Kelliher-Combs, "Curator's Statement" for the exhibition *Points of View VII: Con-Census*, Anchorage Museum of History and Art (2007), as cited in Nadia Jackinsky, "Four Exhibits of Alaska Native Art: Women Artists Breaking Boundaries," *N. Paradoxa* 22 (July 2008): 92.

Additional Works Referenced (Ringlero)

DeRoux, Ken. "Sonya Kelliher-Combs Interview." *Alaska State Museums Bulletin* 16 (Fall 2001).

Favero, Lisa Ann. *Stepping beyond Identity: The Secret's Destination in the Work of Sonya Kelliher-Combs,* Anchorage: Anchorage Museum of History and Art at the Rasmuson Center, 2005.

Freeman, Asia. *Unraveled Secrets, Sonya Kelliher-Combs.* Santa Fe: Institute of American Indian Arts Museum, 2006.

Indke, Dottie. "Sonya Kelliher-Combs," *Southwest Art* 36, no. 8 (January 2007) 28–30.

Rushing, W. Jackson. "Manifest Sovereignty: 'Diversity and Dialogue' at the Eiteljorg Museum." *American Indian Art Magazine* (Summer 2008) 78–88.

Rushing, "Of this Continent." *American Indian Art Magazine* (Winter 2006) 67–76.

Worl, Rosita. "Alaska Natives Today," in *Crossroads of Continents: Cultures of Siberia and Alaska*, 319–25. Ed. William W. Fitzhugh and Aaron Crowell (Washington: Smithsonian Institution Press, 1988).

ELLEGOOD

1. Quoted in Homi K. Bhabha, *The Location of Culture* (New York: Routledge, 1994), 253.

2. Roland Barthes, "The Death of the Author," in *Image-Music-Text*, trans. Stephen Heath (New York: Hill and Wang, 1977).

3. Because her mother was orphaned, Myre and her mother were only able to reclaim their Native or First Nations status relatively recently, in 1997.

4. Richard William Hill, "The Unreadable Present: Nadia Myre & Kent Monkman," *International Contemporary Art* (September 22, 2002).

5. Lynne Cooke, *Ann Hamilton:* tropos, exhibition brochure (New York: Dia Center for the Arts, 1993).

HOLUBIZKY

1. Bernard Smith, *The Spectre of Truganini* (Sydney: Australian Broadcasting Commission, 1980), 10. Turnbull was the historian of the war that saw the annihilation of the Tasmanian Aborigines.

2. The use of "modern" in this context is as an open-ended term. Artists of the mid-nineteenth to early twentieth century can be described as being "formative modern," exploring a language of art that was not predicated on a schooling of master-and-method. "Postmodern" is a debatable term as it has theory in some opposition to stylistic assumptions about modernity, yet it too has no particular form.

3. Dorothy Harley Eber, *Encounters on the Passage: Inuit Meet the Explorers* (University of Toronto Press, 2008), xvii.

4. It is the thesis of Jared Diamond's book *Guns, Germs, and Steel: The Fates of Human Societies* (New York: Norton, 1999).

5. *Grasp Tight the Old Ways* is the title of a 1983 exhibition curated by Jean Blodgett on Inuit art for the Art Gallery of Ontario, Toronto.

6. This and other quotes by the artist cited in this essay are from e-mails, Michael Belmore to the author, March 2009.

7. Etienne Balibar, "The Nation Form: History and Ideology," in *Becoming National: A Reader*, ed. Geoff Eley and Ronald Grigor Suny (New York: Oxford University Press, 1996), 138.

8. Curator Michael Greenwood summarizes the cult of nationalism as "draw[ing] upon those indigenous characteristics to furnish its own particular mythology with emotionally compelling symbols." "Some Nationalist Facets of Canadian Art," *artscanada* 232/233 (Dec. 1979): 69.

9. Olexander Wlasenko, *Michael Belmore: Embankment* (Whitby, ON: Station Gallery, 2009), 8.

10. Ibid.

11. Maps of the Americas appeared in the work of Greg Curnoe (1936–1992), a pro-regional, southern Ontario artist. One mapwork eliminated the United States and abutted Canada to Mexico; in General Idea's printwork *A Mare usque ad Mare* (1987), the geopolitical map of Canada, usually shown in pink as a vestige of the British Empire and Commonwealth, was replaced by the blue of water. The only shoreline, therefore, was the politically drawn 49th parallel. Although not a literal map-work, Carl Beam's (M'chigeeng/Ojibwe) *The North American Iceberg* (1985) has a formative place in Canadian art. From the National Gallery of Canada's website: "[It is a] composition [that] includes images and stenciled phrases drawn from records of current events and from First Nations histories [to] create tenuous connections between the past and the present . . . which suggests a critique of the technological imperative that drives Western civilization, effacing the differences . . . and destroying resistance to that imperative."

12. Joe Bodolai, "Borderlines in Art and Experience," *artscanada* 31 no. 1 (Spring 1974): 65. Bodolai was an expat-American and "new Canadian" at the time. The article was a way of his coming to terms with a "new place" and his sense of "being" in it.

13. I am taking liberties with the term "psychogeography," coined by French theorist Guy Debord in the mid-1950s. He was referring to "inventive" strategies for experiencing and knowing an urban "landscape" and condition.

14. Ralph Waldo Emerson, "The Method of Nature," (1841) published in *Miscellanies; Embracing Nature, Addresses, and Lectures* (Boston: Phillips, Sampson, 1857), 196.

15. It was first shown as part of the installation *Grotesques of the Eastern Woodlands* (2005), but has since been reworked.

16. The Ad Reinhardt (1913–1967) quote appears to be a "bon mot," without a definitive, published source.

17. Likewise, Belmore is by no means the first artist to consider rocks and water together. In the mid-1980s, Canadian Bill Vazan (b. 1933) placed stones in the Li River (Yanshou, South China), as an "action." The purpose was for documentation, as were other comparable found and debris "formations" Vazan carried out during his global trekking. Belmore's work is less literal and demonstrative, although the two artists share the idea of cultural expressions on cosmology.

18. At the time of this writing, Belmore was considering inconspicuously placing one river stone hidden within the installation configuration. The previous, similarly formatted work *Flow* had river stones placed on the surface of the copper, which had been hammered into a cupped form.

19. The most distant source of the Hudson River is several kilometers to the north, at Henderson Lake.

20. One anecdotal-historical moment associated with Lake Tear of the Clouds involves Vice President Theodore Roosevelt, who was at the lake in September 1901 when he received news of President McKinley's grave condition after the assassination attempt two weeks earlier, on September 6.

21. As the majority landowner, the Hudson's Bay Company (HBC) had a major impact on the settling of the Canadian West, and as their core operation changed from fur trading to dry goods retailing at the beginning of the twentieth century, they also entered the immigration business through the Hudson's Bay Overseas Settlement Company. To the company, immigrants meant future customers. In more recent times in Northern Ontario, as the HBC could be the only store in town, the acronym was often expressed as "Here before Christ."

22. Lucy R. Lippard, *The Lure of the Local: Senses of Place in a Multicentered Society* (New York: New Press, 1997), 7, 33.

23. Patricia Deadman, *Terra Incognita* (Guelph, ON: Macdonald Stewart Art Centre, 2007), 23.

RICKARD

1. Christopher Pinney, "Introduction: 'How the Other Half . . .'" in *Photography's Other Histories*, ed. Christopher Pinney and Nicolas Peterson (Chapel Hill, NC: Duke University Press, 2003), 1–16.

2. San Diego Museum of Art press release, "Only Skin Deep: Changing Visions of the American Self, October 1–December 31, 2005," www.tfaoi.com/aa/6aa/6aa110.htm, website hosted by Traditional Fine Arts Organization.

3. Coco Fusco, "Racial Time, Racial Marks, Racial Metaphors" in *Only Skin Deep: Changing Visions of the American Self*, ed. Coco Fusco and Brian Wallis (New York: International Center of Photography and Harry N. Abrams, 2003), 13.

4. The use of sovereignty in this context is not an assertion of a legal status as defined by the judicial system of the United States or Canada. Rather it is used as a marker of continued resistance and self-definition.

5. See Vine Deloria Jr. and Clifford M. Lytle, *The Nations Within: The Past and Future of American Indian Sovereignty* (New York: Pantheon Books, 1984); Oren Lyons, ed., *Exiled in the Land of the Free: Democracy, Indian Nations, and the U.S. Constitution* (Santa Fe, NM: Clear Light Publishers, 1992); and Miriam Jorgensen, ed., *Rebuilding Native Nations: Strategies for Governance and Development* (Tucson: University of Arizona Press, 2007).

6. Lucy R. Lippard, *Mixed Blessings: New Art in a Multicultural America* (New York: Pantheon Books, 1990); Diane Neumaier, ed., *Reframings: New American Feminist Photographies* (Philadelphia: Temple University Press, 1995).

7. Marc Augé, *Non-places: Introduction to an Anthropology of Supermodernity*, trans. John Howe (London: Verso, 1995), 93.

8. Ibid., 96.

9. Donna Haraway, "A Manifesto for Cyborgs: Science, Technology, and Socialist Feminism in the 1980s," reprinted in *The Uncanny: Experiments in Cyborg Culture*, ed. Bruce Grenville (Vancouver: Vancouver Art Gallery, and Arsenal Pulp Press, 2001), 139–81.

10. Marquard Smith, ed., *Stelarc: The Monograph (Electronic Culture: History, Theory, and Practice)* (Cambridge, MA: MIT Press, 2005).

11. Ella Shohat and Robert Stam, *Unthinking Eurocentrism: Multiculturalism and the Media* (New York: Routledge, 1994), 340.

12. Tom Porter, *And Grandma Said . . . Iroquois Teachings: As Passed Down Through the Oral Traditions*, transcribed and ed. Lesley Forester (Philadelphia: Xlibris, 2008), 348–49.

HILL

1. Trinh T. Minh-ha, "Cotton and Iron," in *Out There: Marginalization and Contemporary Cultures*, ed. Russell Ferguson, et al. (New York: New Museum of Contemporary Art, 1990), 330.

2. Gerald McMaster, "Introductions: Mixing It Up," in *Remix: New Modernities in a Post-Indian World*, ed. Joe Baker and Gerald McMaster (Washington, D.C.: National Museum of the American Indian Editions; Phoenix, Arizona: Heard Museum, 2007), 55.

3. I tried unsuccessfully to initiate such a conversation in 1998 with "The Problem with Killing Columbus: Relativism, Ethnic Nationalism and Hybridity," *FUSE Magazine* 21, no. 2 (1998): 7–10.

4. Homi K. Bhabha, *The Location of Culture* (New York: Routledge, 1994).

5. Jimmie Durham, "Ni' Go Tlunh A Doh Ka," in *A Certain Lack of Coherence* (London: Kala Press, 1993), 110. The first text that I am aware of to treat the essential unreality of the Indian is Roy Harvey Pearce's brilliant book *The Savages of America: A Study of the Indian and the Idea of Civilization* (Baltimore: Johns Hopkins Press, 1953), revised in 1988 as *Savagism and Civilization: A Study of the Indian and the American Mind* (Berkeley: University of California Press). Also influential was Robert E. Berkhofer, Jr., *The White Man's*

Indian: Images of the American Indian from Columbus to the Present (New York: Vintage Books, 1978). Perhaps as important, although its subject was "the Orient" rather than the Americas, was Edward Said's *Orientalism* (New York: Vintage, 1979), which brought the critique of colonial thought into engagement with Marxist theories of ideology and poststructuralist discourse theory, through the author's interest in Antonio Gramsci and Michel Foucault respectively.

6. George Boas and Arthur O. Lovejoy, *Primitivism and Related Ideas in Antiquity* (Baltimore: Johns Hopkins Press, 1935), 10.

7. Ibid., 287.

8. See George Boas, *Essays on Primitivism and Related Ideas in the Middle Ages* (Baltimore: Johns Hopkins Press, 1948); Richard Bernheimer, *Wild Men in the Middle Ages: a Study in Art, Sentiment, and Demonology* (Cambridge, MA: Harvard University Press, 1952); Edward Joseph Dudely and Maximillian E. Novak, eds., *The Wild Man Within: An Image in Western Thought from the Renaissance to Romanticism* (Pittsburgh: University of Pittsburgh Press, 1972).

9. Susi Colin, "The Wild Man and the Indian in Early Sixteenth Century Book Illustration," in *Indians and Europe: An Interdisciplinary Collection of Essays*, ed. C. F. Feest (Aachen, Germany: Edition Herodot, Rader Verlag, 1987), 5–36.

10. Durham, "An Open Letter: Or Recent Developments in the American Indian Movement/International Treaty Council" (1980) and "Trying to See Clearly" (1978) in *A Certain Lack of Coherence: Writings on Art and Cultural Politics* ed. Jean Fisher (London: Kala Press, 1993, original 1980), 55, 37.

11. Durham, "American Indian Culture: Traditionalism and Spiritualism in a Revolutionary Struggle," (1974) in *A Certain Lack of Coherence*, 4.

12. Durham, "The Ground Has Been Covered" (1988) in *A Certain Lack of Coherence*, 137.

13. Ibid., 136.

14. Laura Mulvey, Dirk Snauwaert, and Mark Alice Durant, "Interview with Dirk Snauwaert," in *Jimmie Durham* (London: Phaidon, 1995), 13.

15. Durham, "A Certain Lack of Coherence" (1988), in *A Certain Lack of Coherence*, 146.

16. Durham, "Ni' Go Tlunh A Doh Ka," 108.

17. Durham, *Columbus Day* (Albuquerque, NM: West End Press, 1983), 84.

18. Michael Taussig, *Mimesis and Alterity: A Particular History of the Senses* (New York: Routledge, 1993), 78.

19. Ibid., 249.

20. Russell Means with Marvin Wolf, *Where White Men Fear to Tread: The Autobiography of Russell Means* (New York: St. Martin's Press, 1995), 110.

21. Adolf Hitler, *Mein Kampf*, trans. Ralph Manheim (Boston: Houghton Mifflin, 1943), 284.

22. Chadwick Allen, *Blood Narrative: Indigenous Identity in American Indian and Maori Literary and Activist Texts* (Durham, NC: Duke University Press, 2002), 178.

23. Allen, "Blood (and) Memory," *American Literature* 71, no. 1 (March 1999): 95.

24. Ibid., n. 112.

25. Ibid., 95.

26. U.S. Department of the Interior, "Indian Arts and Crafts Act of 1990," www.doi.gov/iacb/act.html.

27. U.S. Department of the Interior, "Violations of the Indian Arts and Crafts Act," www.doi.gov/iacb/file.html.

28. See Joanne Barker "Indian™ U.S.A.," *Wicazo Sa Review* 18, no. 1 (Spring 2003): 25–79; Gail K. Sheffield, *The Arbitrary Indian: The Indian Arts and Crafts Act of 1990* (Norman: University of Oklahoma Press, 1997); and Kay WalkingStick, "Democracy Inc.: Kay WalkingStick on Indian Law," *Artforum International*, no. 30 (November 1991): 20–21, reprinted as "Indian Arts and Crafts Act: Counterpoint," *Akwe:kon Journal* 11, nos. 3–4 (1994): 115–17.

Exhibition Checklist

SONYA KELLIHER-COMBS

Common Thread, 2008–10 (p. 23)
    Reindeer and sheep rawhide, nylon thread
    Variable dimensions
    Collection of the Artist

Cream Walrus Family Portrait I and *II*, 2009–10
    Acrylic polymer, paper, nylon thread, fabric
    162.5 x 101.6 cm each
    Collection of the artist

Salmon Walrus Family Portrait with Trim, 2009–10 (p. 40)
    Acrylic polymer, walrus stomach, paper, reindeer fur, nylon
    thread, glass beads, archival ink, fabric
    177.8 x 101.6 cm
    Collection of the artist

Gold Walrus Family Portrait I and *II*, 2010
    Acrylic polymer, walrus stomach, paper, porcupine quill,
    nylon thread, fabric
    106.7 x 101.6 cm each
    Collection of the artist

Pink Walrus Family Portrait, 2010
    Acrylic polymer, paper, reindeer fur, nylon thread, glass
    beads archival ink, fabric
    162.5 x 101.6 cm
    Collection of the artist

Small Secrets, 2009 (p. 43)
    Walrus stomach, human hair, glass beads, nylon thread
    Variable dimensions
    Collection of the artist

Brand series, 2009 (cover, p. 24)
    Marten skin, reindeer fur, seal skin, sea lion skin, tanned
    moose hide, polar bear fur, walrus stomach, seal intes-
    tine, reindeer rawhide, sheep rawhide, porcupine quill,
    feathers, human hair, acrylic polymer, cotton cloth, glass
    beads, metal grommets and eyelets, nylon thread
    Variable dimensions
    Collection of the artist

Shedding Skin, 2010 (p. 26)
    Needles, nylon and cotton thread
    Variable dimensions
    Collection of the artist

NADIA MYRE

The Scar Project, 2005–present (p. 55)
    More than 500 canvases and stories written on paper
    25.4 x 25.4 x 5.1 cm each; 20.3 x 27.9 cm each
    Collection of the artist

Landscape of Sorrow, 2009 (pp. 59, 61)
    6 canvases, cotton thread
    15.2 x 213.4 cm each
    Collection of the artist

Scarscapes, 2009 (pp. 27, 52)
    Glass beads, cotton thread
    5 works, 35.6 x 10.2 cm each
    Collection of the artist

Scarscapes, 2009
    5 digital prints on paper
    101.6 x 182.9 cm each
    Collection of the artist

Inkanatatation, 2004 (p. 14)
    Digital video
    1:27 min.
    Collection of the artist

MICHAEL BELMORE

Shorelines, 2006 (pp. 69, 70, 71)
    Hammered copper
    213.4 x 182.9 cm
    Collection of the artist

Origins, 2009 (p. 74)
    Hammered copper
    30.5 x 30.5 cm
    Collection of the artist

Dark Water, 2009–10 (pp. 66, 75, 76)
    Hammered copper, steel
    304.8 x 487.7 cm
    Collection of the artist

Flux, 2010 (p. 72)
    River stones, gold leaf
    Floor installation, 243.8 x 274.3 cm
    Collection of the artist

KC ADAMS

Cyborg Hybrids—New York Series, 2009
    Digital prints
    50.8 x 35.6 cm each
    Collection of the artist

    Cyborg Hybrid Alli (p. 115)
    Cyborg Hybrid Cody (p. 86)
    Cyborg Hybrid Donna (p. 32)
    Cyborg Hybrid Teresa (p. 115)
    Cyborg Hybrid Tom (p. 34)
    Cyborg Hybrid Renzo (p. 87)
    Cyborg Hybrid Yatika (p. 32)

ROSALIE FAVELL

Facing the Camera, 2008–present
    Digital prints
    61 x 50.8 cm each
    Collection of the artist

    Barry Ace (p. 117)
    Rosalie Favell (p. 84)
    Candice Hopkins (p. 85)
    Alex Janvier (p. 85)
    Nadia Myre (p. 117)
    Ron Noganosh (p. 101)
    Edward Poitras (p. 85)
    Ryan Rice (p. 33)
    Tania Willard (p. 85)

TERRANCE HOULE

Photos by Jarusha Brown
Urban Indian Series, 2007
    Eight digital C-prints (pp. 37, 78, 90, 91, 107, 119)
    35.6 x 27.9 cm each
    Collection of the artist

Metrosexual Indian, 2005 (p. 37)
    Super 8 and digital video
    4 min.
    Collection of the artist

ARTHUR RENWICK

Mask, 2006
    Edition of 3
    Digital prints
    119.4 x 114.3 cm each
    Collection of the artist

    Carla (title page)
    Danny (p. 83)
    Eden (p. 30)
    Fernando (p. 30)
    Michelle (p. 83)
    Tom (p. 80)
    Jani (p. 20)
    Thomas (p. 121)

SARAH SENSE

Karl 1, 2009 (p. 39)
    Digital prints on paper and mylar, artist tape
    121.9 x 243.8 cm
    Collection of the artist

Karl 2, 2009 (pp. 93, 94)
    Digital prints on paper and mylar, artist tape
    121.9 x 243.8 cm
    Collection of the artist

Karl 3, 2009 (pp. 38, 93, 123)
    Digital prints on paper and mylar, artist tape
    121.9 x 243.8 cm
    Collection of the artist

Contributors

Kathleen Ash-Milby (Navajo) is an associate curator of contemporary art at NMAI's George Gustav Heye Center in New York. She earned her master of arts from the University of New Mexico in Native American art history. Her tenure at the National Museum of the American Indian began with a research position (1993–99), during which she assisted with the NMAI's exhibition and publication *Woven by the Grandmothers* (1996). She has worked as an independent curator, writer, and consultant and organized numerous contemporary art exhibitions as the curator and co-director of the American Indian Community House Gallery in New York (2000–05). She returned to the NMAI in 2005, after which she organized the exhibition *Off the Map: Landscape in the Native Imagination* (2007) and edited the accompanying publication. She was also the co-curator, with Truman Lowe, for *Edgar Heap of Birds: Most Serene Republics*, a public art installation and collateral project for the 52nd International Art Exhibition/Venice Biennale (2007), and served as editor and contributing author of its publication (2009).

Anne Ellegood joined the Armand Hammer Museum of Art and Culture Center, Los Angeles, in May 2009 as senior curator. Before that, she was curator of contemporary art at the Hirshhorn Museum and Sculpture Garden in Washington, DC, from 2005 to 2009. Ellegood was the New York based curator for Californian Peter Norton's collection and, from 1998 to 2003, she was associate curator at the New Museum of Contemporary Art in New York. At the Hirshhorn, she organized solo shows of the work of artists Jim Lambie, Amy Sillman, and Terence Gower. Group exhibitions include *The Uncertainty of Objects and Ideas: Recent Sculpture* (2002) and *Realisms* (2008), the second installation of a two-part exhibition titled *The Cinema Effect: Reality, Illusion, and the Moving Image*, coorganized with Kristen Hileman. Ellegood has contributed texts to a number of catalogues and written for such publications as *Artforum* and *Art Press*. She received her master of arts from the Center for Curatorial Studies (CCS) at Bard College. She has since taught critical theory and contemporary art seminars at Bard's CCS; Rhode Island School of Design; School of the Visual Arts, George Washington University; and The Center for the Study of Modern Art, University of Illinois, at The Phillips Collection.

 **John Haworth** (Cherokee) has been director of the NMAI's George Gustav Heye Center in New York since 1995. Under his leadership, the museum developed the Diker Pavilion for Native Arts and Cultures, which opened in 2006, and will open a major collections-based exhibition titled *Infinity of Nations* in 2010. He serves on NMAI's Exhibition Assessment Group, its Modern and Contemporary Native Art Initiative team, and the Director's Roundtable. He has been a featured speaker and panelist at statewide, regional, and national arts conferences and has written extensively on cultural and museum issues. Haworth previously served as assistant commissioner for cultural institutions at the NYC Department of Cultural Affairs and taught arts management and cultural policy at New York University. Haworth received an MBA from Columbia University, where he was also designated a Revson Fellow on the Future of New York City.

Richard William Hill (Cree) is a curator, critic, art historian, and assistant professor of art history at York University, Toronto, Ontario, where he has taught since 2002. As a curator at the Art Gallery of Ontario, Hill oversaw the museum's first substantial effort to include North American Aboriginal art and ideas in permanent-collection galleries. He also curated *Kazuo Nakamura: A Human Measure* at the Art Gallery of Ontario in 2004 and co-curated, with Jimmie Durham, *The American West* at Compton Verney, Warwickshire, England, in 2005. His most recent curatorial project is *The World Upside Down*, which originated at the Walter Phillips Gallery at The Banff Centre in 2006 and is currently on tour. Hill's essays on art have appeared in numerous books, exhibition catalogues and periodicals. He has a long association with the art magazine *FUSE*, for which he served as a member of the board, was on the editorial committee, and remains a contributing editor. Hill is currently writing a book on the problem of agency in the art of Jimmie Durham, the subject of his PhD thesis.

Ihor Holubizky is an art and cultural historian, a curator at the McMaster Museum of Art in Hamilton, Ontario, and a doctoral candidate at the University of Queensland, Australia. He has held curatorial positions in public galleries in Canada and Australia over the past thirty years and has lectured internationally on a broad range of cultural issues. In addition, he has written on a wide range of topics over the past twenty years. He has most recently contributed essays to the publications *Futurism and After: David Burliuk, 1882–1967* (2008); *Mischa Kuball, In Progress* (2009); *Shaun Gladwell: Videowork* (2007); and collaborated with Dr. Jeanne Randolph on her book, *Ethics of Luxury: Materialism and Imagination* (2007).

Jolene Rickard (Tuscarora) is an associate professor in the History of Art and Visual Studies department at Cornell University. She received a PhD from the State University of New York at Buffalo, a master of science degree from Buffalo State College, a bachelor of fine and applied arts from the Rochester Institute of Technology, and has studied at the London College of Printing in England. Theoretically engaged in issues relevant to post- and neo-coloniality, Rickard is an artist, curator, and historian concentrating on the aesthetic practice of First Nations and indigenous peoples within a global context. Her photographic installations have been exhibited at such venues as the Canadian Museum of Civilization in Quebec; Barbican Centre in London; Joseph Gross Gallery at the University of Arizona in Tucson; Ansel Adams Center for Photography in San Francisco; Houston Center for Photography; and Exit Art in New York City.

Aleta Ringlero (Pima) is an art historian and former project director of Native American Public Programs at the Smithsonian's National Museum of Natural History. Since 1999, Ringlero has provided the direction and curatorial leadership for the establishment of the fine art collections of Casino Arizona at McKellips in Scottsdale, Arizona, and River Rock Casino, Healdsburg, California (2002–06). She regularly contributes to *American Indian*, the member publication of the National Museum of the American Indian. Her recent articles focus on art by Fritz Scholder, Harry Fonseca, Virgil Ortiz, and Nora Naranjo-Morse. Ringlero's contributions to academic journals, exhibition catalogues, and subject encyclopedias include: "Simeon Schwemberger: Observations of 'Big Eyes'" in *Place and Native American Indian History and Culture* (2007); and "Prairie Pinups: Reconsidering Historic Portraits of American Indian Women" for the touring exhibition *Only Skin Deep: Changing Visions of the American Self* (2003), for which she also served on the curatorial team. Ringlero holds degrees in art history and humanities with specializations in contemporary indigenous art history and nineteenth-century art and photography.

For Further Reading

Casey, Edward S. *Earth-Mapping: Artists Reshaping Landscape.* Minneapolis: University of Minnesota Press, 2005.

Deadman, Patricia. *Terra Incognita: Mary Anne Barkhouse and Michael Belmore.* Guelph, Ontario: Macdonald Stewart Art Centre, 2007.

Deloria, Philip J. *Indians in Unexpected Places.* Lawrence: University Press of Kansas, 2004.

Fusco, Coco, and Brian Wallis, eds. *Only Skin Deep: Changing Visions of the American Self.* New York: Harry N. Abrams in association with the International Center of Photography, 2003.

Gillespie, Sandy. "Sonya Kelliher-Combs: Secrets." In *Diversity and Dialogue: The Eiteljorg Fellowship for Native American Fine Art,* ed. James H. Nottage, 61–75. Indianapolis: Eiteljorg Museum of American Indians and Western Art; Seattle: University of Washington Press, 2007.

Grenville, Bruce, ed. *The Uncanny: Experiments in Cyborg Culture.* Vancouver: Vancouver Art Gallery in partnership with Arsenal Pulp Press, 2001.

Harper, Kenn. *Give Me My Father's Body: The Life of Minik, the New York Eskimo.* South Royalton, VT: Steerforth Press, 2000.

Lupton, Ellen. *Skin: Surface, Substance, and Design.* New York: Cooper-Hewitt National Design Museum and Princeton Architectural Press, 2002.

Meier, Rhonda, et al. *Nadia Myre: Cont(r)act.* Montreal: Dark Horse Productions, 2004.

O'Bryan, C. Jill. *Carnal Art: Orlan's Refacing.* Minneapolis: University of Minnesota Press, 2005.

O'Donnell, Joan Kathryn, and Jonathan Batkin, eds. *About Face: Self-Portraits by Native American, First Nations and Inuit Artists.* Santa Fe: Wheelwright Museum of the American Indian, 2006.

Sonya Kelliher-Combs, *Lime Walrus Family Portrait*, 2008. Acrylic polymer, nylon thread, paper, walrus stomach, 33 x 33 cm. Collection of John Rolston.

Starn, Orin. *Ishi's Brain: In Search of America's Last 'Wild' Indian.* New York: Norton, 2004.

Taylor, Mark C. *Hiding.* Chicago: University of Chicago Press, 1997.

Wakeham, Pauline. *Taxidermic Signs: Reconstructing Aboriginality.* Minneapolis: University of Minnesota Press, 2008.

Acknowledgments

It is a privilege to acknowledge, on behalf of the National Museum of the American Indian, the many people and organizations who have contributed to the exhibition and publication of *HIDE: Material and Metaphor*. Projects such as *HIDE* involve a multitude of people to be a success, but they start with the artists who have created the intriguing and intelligent work featured in the exhibition and the publication. We therefore must first thank Sonya Kelliher-Combs, Nadia Myre, and Michael Belmore, whose art seeded the ideas explored in *HIDE*. The photographic artists added an essential dimension to the broader concepts in the exhibition; we are grateful for the participation of Arthur Renwick, KC Adams, Sarah Sense, Terrance Houle, and Rosalie Favell. Thanks to Myre's gallery, Art Mûr (Montreal), and Renwick's gallery, Leo Kamen Gallery (Toronto), for their time and thoughtful assistance in many aspects of the project, and to the Canada Council for the Arts' support of Michael Belmore's work.

In our mission to provide a broader context and understanding in the publication, we included images of the work of many additional artists. Many thanks to Erica Lord, Rebecca Belmore, Skawennati, Jason Lewis, Jason Lujan, Adrian Stimson, Zig Jackson, ORLAN, Ann Hamilton, Janine Antoni and Luhring Augustine Gallery, Lucio Fontana and Gagosian Gallery, Byron Kim and Max Protetch Gallery, Dinh Q. Lê and 10 Chancery Lane Gallery, and the estates of Eva Hesse and Hannah Wilke.

We are grateful to our guest writers who provided cogent reflections and thoughtful analysis of the artists' work: Aleta Ringlero, Anne Ellegood, Ihor Holubizky, and Jolene Rickard. Thanks also to Richard William Hill for his challenging and insightful essay on the representation of Indian skin. We appreciate your time and valuable contributions to the publication.

It always a pleasure to work with contemporary artists at the NMAI, but projects like this, which, challenge our audiences, would not be realized without the critical support of the museum's director, Kevin Gover, and the advocacy of senior staff, including Tim Johnson, John Haworth, and Peter Brill. *HIDE* is part of a larger initiative to expand our contemporary art exhibitions, scholarship, and program-

ming. We thank the Modern and Contemporary Native Arts Program staff for their encouragement and support, including Paul Chaat Smith, Rebecca Trautmann, Jennifer Miller, Lesley Devrouax, and consultants Suzanne Delehanty and Simon Brascoupe. The NMAI's contemporary art program has received generous support from the Ford Foundation.

Thank you to the project team: Betsy Gordon, Jennifer Miller, Barbara Suhr, Susanna Stieff, Kate Johnson, Robert Mastrangelo, Maria McWilliams, Lucia DeRespinis, Johanna Gorelick, Shawn Termin, Ann Marie Sekeres, Quinn Bradley, Rick Pelasara, John Richardson, Stacey Jones, Jason Wigfield, and the cultural interpreter and visitor services staff.

Much appreciation also to the NMAI Publications Office team who worked on this project: Terence Winch, Tanya Thrasher, Steve Bell, Ann Kawasaki, and contract editors Amy Pickworth, Liz Hill, and Jane McAllister. A special thanks to Alexandra Harris, who worked closely and tirelessly with me to shape and fine-tune this publication. It was a pleasure to work with her astute sensibility . . . and patience.

We graciously tip our hat to Rachel Griffin, contract research assistant, who helped us wrangle a million details and kept us sane. Thanks also to Lynne Altstatt and the staff of the Vine Deloria, Jr. Library, NMAI, who must have sent more than one hundred books to me in New York and processed numerous interlibrary loan requests throughout the research and development of the project.

For the rights and permissions related to the *Jaws* sidebar (p. 65) we would like to especially thank Wendy Benchley, Richard Dreyfuss, and Virginia Shaw. Thanks also to the collectors of the *Walrus Family Portraits* reproduced in the publication: John Rolston, Donna Goldsmith, and John Letourneau.

As the project curator, I would like to extend personal thanks to some individuals outside of the NMAI who nonetheless provided support for the project as sounding boards, cheerleaders, and professional peers: Patsy Phillips, Ryan Rice, and Samantha Ferguson (Institute of American Indian Arts, Santa Fe), Jeffrey Gibson, Ellen Taubman, Kate Morris, Carolyn Kastner, Charlotte Townsend-Gault, Melissa Martens (Museum of Jewish Heritage, New York), Vanessa Visconti, Jacqueline Severing, and, last but not ever least, my family, Edward Ash-Milby and sons Nathan and Wyatt.

Kathleen Ash-Milby, Associate Curator, NMAI

Credits

Cover, photo by Kevin G. Smith; title page, courtesy of Arthur Renwick and Leo Kamen Gallery; 14 (top), 19, photo by Ernest Amoroso, NMAI; 20, courtesy of Arthur Renwick and Leo Kamen Gallery; 21 (bottom), courtesy of the artist and Franco Soffiantino Arte Contemporanea; 23–26, photos by Kevin G. Smith; 30, courtesy of Arthur Renwick and Leo Kamen Gallery; 31, courtesy ORLAN and Galerie Michel Rein, Paris; 40, 42–43, photos by Kevin G. Smith; 47, Philadelphia Museum of Art: Purchased with funds contributed by Mr. and Mrs. Leonard Korman, Mr. and Mrs. Keith Sachs, Marion Boulton Stroud, Mr. and Mrs. Bayard T. Storey, and with other various funds, 1990. Photo by Graydon Wood; 48, 50–51, photos by Kevin G. Smith; 56 (top), courtesy of the artist and Max Protetch Gallery; 56 (bottom), courtesy of the artist and Luhring Augustine Gallery, New York; 59, photo by Lee Stalsworth; 62 (bottom), photo by Thibault Jeanson, courtesy of Ann Hamilton Studio; 64, photo by Kevin G. Smith; 65, courtesy of Universal Studios Licensing LLLP, © 1974, renewed 2002 Winifred W. Benchley, courtesy of Richard Dreyfuss and Virginia Shaw; 69–71, photos by Michael Cullen; 79, © 2008 Comedy Partners. All Rights Reserved; 80, 83, courtesy of Arthur Renwick and Leo Kamen Gallery; 88, courtesy of Adrian Stimson; 89, courtesy of Zig Jackson; 92 (top), courtesy of 10 Chancery Lane Gallery & Dinh Q. Lê; 100, courtesy of Paramount Pictures/Photofest; 108, photo by Sheryl Maree Reily; 109, photos by Kathleen Ash-Milby; 110, photo by Rosalie Favell; 111, photos by Nadia Myre; 112, photo by Michael Belmore; 113, photos by Kathleen Ash-Milby; 114, photo by Scott Stephens; 116, photo by Rosalie Favell; 118, photo by Jarusha Brown; 120, photo by Nadya Kwadibens, Red Works Studio, © Nadya Kwadibens and Arthur Renwick; 122, photo by Renzo Spirit Buffalo; 123, photos by Kathleen Ash-Milby; 130 (top), photo by Anthony Two Moons; 130 (bottom), courtesy of the Hammer Museum, photo by Andre Vippolis; 131, photo by Anthony Two Moons; 132 (top), photo by Michael Mitchell; 132 (middle), courtesy of Jolene Rickard; 132 (bottom), courtesy of the National Anthropological Archives, Smithsonian Institution; 133, photo by Kevin G. Smith.